T0375623

HE is
WATCHING

DIANE KURTZ CALABRESE

WESTBOW
PRESS®
A DIVISION OF THOMAS NELSON
& ZONDERVAN

WestBow Press books may be ordered through booksellers or by contacting:

WestBow Press
A Division of Thomas Nelson & Zondervan
1663 Liberty Drive
Bloomington, IN 47403
www.westbowpress.com
844-714-3454

All Bible citations are from the New American Bible (NAB).

Hartdegen & Hickey. (1986). The St. Joseph Edition no. 62 of The New American Bible. Catholic Book Publishing Co.

ISBN: 979-8-3850-2366-0 (sc)
ISBN: 979-8-3850-2365-3 (e)

Library of Congress Control Number: 2024907597

Print information available on the last page.

WestBow Press rev. date: 5/13/2024

He Is Watching by Diane Calabrese is a compelling and spiritually enriching guide that navigates the virtues of leading a good life, addresses the nuanced differences among sins, and outlines the righteous path in alignment with Christian principles. Diane's insightful exploration into societal values prompts readers to reevaluate their lives and strive for a more virtuous existence. What sets this book apart is the inclusion of multiple opinions by clergy, offering a diverse range of perspectives that enrich the discussion on Christian living. Her poignant reflections on the proximity of the end times provide a timely wake-up call, encouraging readers to assess their preparedness to meet Christ. I highly recommend this thought-provoking book to anyone seeking a deeper understanding of Christian living and a renewed commitment to a life of purpose and virtue.

Miguel Bustillos, pastor, exorcist, and Christian counselor

Breaking free from the limits of traditional literature, *He Is Watching* embarks on a profound exploration of the realms of sin, virtue, and the Christian way of life. Calabrese magnificently balances shared values with a poignant emphasis on significant differences, tracing the broad consequences of evolving societal norms on families, schools, and nations. Drawing insights from the Bible, clergy interviews, and the author's experiences in health care, *He Is Watching* exhorts us to ponder on the questions regarding our preparedness for potential end times and creates an engaging tapestry that invites readers on a contemplative journey through life's profound questions and their enduring impact.

Aldrin D. Nacu, LPT, MATh, MPM, BA in philosophy, MA in theology, MA in pastoral ministry, educator, Catholic writer, and editor

A thought-provoking book that addresses modern challenges through personal faith. I love the way Diane combines religious ideas, her own experiences, and conversations with religious leaders to explore faith, choices, and moral rights and wrongs.

Prof. Krishna N. Sharma, vice-chancellor, St. Louis University, Cameroon; former vice-chancellor, Victoria University, Uganda; best-selling author; world record holder; and TEDx speaker

Let's consider for a minute the probability of any one of us being born. First our parents had to meet and fall in love. Then they had to begin to try to get pregnant. Next only one in millions of sperm would fertilize one of five hundred thousand eggs. This fertilized egg would be you. The best estimate would be one in 400 trillion odds for your being born. Lucky, fortunate, blessed—all these words and more sum up our being. Diane Calabrese's new book is excellent in helping each of us fully live our lives. We are to take each day and wring the very most out of it while making a positive difference in the world we inhabit. Each of us needs to answer the question, "Will it matter that I was?

Rev. Dr. John H. Krahn, author, Lutheran minister

In this book Diane truly gives us a detailed and versatile look at some long-time biblical, fundamental beliefs. So eye opening and refreshing to read several theological and world views from leaders of all different denominations. If you want to stretch your understanding and add balance to your belief system, this is a great read.

Rev. Kevin Hartman, pastor, care coordinator

He Is Watching is an eye-opening book of spiritual guidance and uplifting ways to see ourselves. Why are humans curious about how their faith in humankind and their right to choose the teachings of how God and the Bible are manifested in our hearts? How and why? Included at the end of each chapter, there are questions that will challenge our knowledge and help us develop a stronger understanding of what faith, trust, hope, and fear are and—how evil can turn us away from our faith. Satan can fool us, but God's teachings show us the way, life, and truth. You will want to explore this informative and gratifying piece of literature—a book for all ages to understand.

Crystal Miles Gauthier, author/writer, CEO of C & J Promotions and Marketing Agency

He Is Watching by Diane Kurtz Calabrese is a most intriguing book! It will keep you turning pages to see what comfort the author has to present you with. Her work is well-researched and backed up with ministers, pastors, and other ministry specialists. The book is easy to read and leaves you sometimes uneasy with questions asked of the reader of their faith. I strongly recommend *He Is Watching*. Your faith will be both comforted and challenged. This reader's was.

Sheri Adams, Christian, author, artist

Compelling and enlightening book that provides moral clarity to an increasingly confusing time in our culture. Calabrese illuminates a wide range of topics, but in the end faith in God, true remorse, and actions that beget forgiveness remain the pillars of Christian belief. A panel of clergy add their voices to a number of ecclesiastical questions that laypeople and other readers will find revealing. A must read for anyone who is seeking answers to universal questions.

Dan Mariani, author of many books, including *Exploring the Boundaries of Time-Space and Our Lives*

Diane digs deep into the UFO issue and how it relates to the Bible. She is what I call a *truth seeker*! This book looks at an issue that for a long time has been overlooked by powers in control of our daily lives!

Kenneth Dudley, UFO investigator

A deep dive into faith and society that pushes you to reevaluate.

Nicole Mullaney, author; script supervisor for TV, film, and commercials; award-winning romance novelist, Pen It Publications

This book is dedicated to Jesus Christ,
my best friend,
my Lord and Savior.

I'd like to extend a special thank you to all the clergy who participated in the personal interviews with me on some of these controversial issues facing society today:

Father C. George Mary Claret
Reverend Kevin Hartman
Reverend Angela Heil
Reverend Dr. John H. Krahn
Reverend Kenneth W. Boggs
Reverend Joseph Pennella
Reverend Miguel Bustillos

My intention for this book is to bring to light the evils that do exist and perhaps always have existed in the world but have become for whatever reason more transparent in society. It feels like human ethics has declined, resulting in weakened morals and more disrespect, to the point where society has really crossed the line into a place of evil that I'm not sure it can return from.

I do know we cannot do it without God.

CONTENTS

INTRODUCTION

In their greed they will exploit you with fabrications,
but from of old their condemnation has not been
idle, and their destruction does not sleep.
— 2 Peter 2:3

He Is Watching is a book regarding the virtues of leading a good life. What are the differences among sins? What are we called to do? What is deemed righteous in society, and what is not in alignment with living a Christian life? Last, are you prepared for the end of time? We may be closer than you think to that day than ever before. Whether we are there or not, we never know when our last day on earth will be. Are you ready to meet Christ?

There are many acceptable practices and ways of living among the various religions, cultures, and countries of the world. Most, I believe, have more in common than not; however, we do have very distinct differences that affect the way all individuals make choices regarding themselves and society at large. These decisions are both personally and politically based, and they affect our families, our public schools, our cities, our countries, and the world. As the world has become more liberal, the rules have changed across the board. We don't value the same things as in the past, and this is true in most countries and religions—although some are more subtle than others.

America alone has become an entirely different country from only 250 years ago, when the United States gained its independence from Great Britain. The main reason citizens fled Great Britain was for religious freedom. Paganism was the primary religion in Great Britain. In many areas, Catholics were being persecuted, and in other areas Protestants were the ones being targeted. People fled to America for the freedom to practice their choice of religion, among other freedoms. This is a *fact*, but it is not taught in our public schools anymore. The idea and belief in Jesus Christ, our Lord and Savior, has become a pastime understanding in media and society in general today. To have faith in Christ is to follow Him, to essentially do what He would do. That exact understanding among Christians is no longer practiced.

Society has come so far yet has lost so much. There have been good changes as well as not-so-good changes. This book focuses less on class and more on the values and morals of the people at large—reflective of the Bible and clergy from different denominations as well as my own insight and reflections. This book includes detailed data from the author's first-person interviews with clergy as well as scripture, peer-reviewed research, and the firsthand experiences of this author in the health-care industry.

The book also incorporates stories and books of the mystics, the book of Enoch, and ancient aliens (the fallen angels) as well as other phenomena that are profoundly important. This includes the testimonies of people who had near-death or out-of-body experiences, witnessed paranormal activity, or saw visions or apparitions of the Blessed Mother.

Today's core hot topics—including abortion, sex trafficking, and the use of adrenochrome—and the various kinds of sins, including greed, jealousy, envy, and emotional as well as physical wrongdoings, play key roles in the dogma and lifestyles of the classes and have profoundly corrupted society and impacted lifestyles. It begs the questions, Where are we as people? Where are we as a nation? Where are we as a world? What are we doing? Where are we going? Where did we come from? And why were we put on this earth? What is life's ultimate purpose, and how does God fit into all of this?

Furthermore, how will we be judged after death? How does God see it? We all have crosses to bear, and many of us ask, "Why is mine so difficult?" Who's responsible? Who's taking responsibility? Who's to blame? The questions and lists of gripes and grudges go on and on. Are we addressing these moral issues, and where does this really need to start? From what I see, it's like anything else—it needs to start right in our own homes. Let's see what the research outcomes are, what the Bible says, hear my first-person interviews with Christian clergy, my thoughts, reflections, conclusion—and, above all, lasting thoughts you can ponder.

One

THE DIFFERENCE BETWEEN BELIEF AND FAITH

> Now to him who can strengthen you, according to my
> gospel and the proclamation of Jesus Christ, according to the
> revelation of the mystery kept secrets for long ages, but now
> manifested through the prophetic writings and, according to
> the command of the eternal God, made known to all nationals
> to bring about the obedience of faith. —Romans 16:25–26

Believing in God is not the same as having *faith*—as having faith is not the same as *trusting* or *knowing*. When we believe something is true, we have hope. Our gut tells us something is probably true, that it must be true. Saying we believe in God can be as cliché as predicting the weather or the outcome of a circumstance. We may feel there *has* to be a higher power, someone who is in charge of the universe. Even Satan and all his demons *believe* God exists or they wouldn't be trying so hard to win over souls to gain the ultimate power of the universe. Think about it. However, Satan and his demons do not have faith.

Faith is about believing what you cannot see, and you betray yourself

1

when you do not act on faith. Faith includes the will—it is the trust and commitment that result in a change of behavior. Faith is consummated as an act of obedience in response to believing; it involves a decision. Faith calls for action, not silence. Faith alone does not save. You must act. You must be willing to sacrifice yourself because evil prevails when the good do nothing.

> Faith by itself, if it is not accompanied by action, is dead. Show me your faith without deeds, and I will show you my faith by my deeds. You believe that there is one God. Good! Even the demons believe that—and shudder. (James 2:17–20)

Faith is a whole different level of *belief.* When we have faith, we not only believe God exists but live as if God were part of our everyday lives. Those with faith spread a different kind of light into the universe. Those who believe in God have kindness in them and live good lives—but do they live for God? Maybe, maybe not. They may do good needs here and there. They may show gratitude, good virtue, and righteousness, which is extremely important. We cannot do without that.

In faith, we consciously live according to the teachings of the biblical scripture. That doesn't mean we don't make mistakes. We absolutely do, but when we ask for forgiveness, we mean it. The remorse is real, not artificial. An apology and an act of confession with a priest need to be sincere for the forgiveness to happen. As a faithful person, you want to go to heaven. We want to please God because we *know* He exists. Faith is a dedication to Jesus Christ. It is a dedication to His teachings, trying to help others, and servicing Him in doing so. This is a routine act of faith—knowing you are serving the Lord and offering your virtuous deeds up to the Lord and serving Him in a way that is above and beyond a selfish intention. Many people do virtuous deeds and live a good life, but are the underlying intentions always selfless? All actions begin with a thought, and that thought turns into action based upon our intentions, which will influence the outcome. Our intention is the cause the action that is taken, which then produces an effect. When you are faithful to God, your intentions are in alignment with the effect. It is sincere, genuine thought that leads to a positive effect on the universe at large. It is so important to be conscious of that in all our decisions. Ask yourself, *Why am I pursuing this? What is the reason? What is my intention? Is it for a positive cause and effect?* Most important of all, pray. Pray for the grace of trusting your inner self to make the right choices.

People shudder when asked direct questions, especially when they can't give a truthful response. I will be devoting a chapter to deception and lies later in the book, but know that what you say matters. Everything matters.

People are human; we make mistakes. We have feelings, and those feelings get in the way of many decisions, including the choices of words we use. Many conversations are difficult. People shy away from confrontational conversations. They will dismiss them as abrasive or deflect the discussion onto another topic or person to cast blame. But truth is the illumination of pure light—it transforms you. Take the time to listen to what others are saying in the midst of what you may not want to hear because, sometimes, it needs to be heard. Most often it is coming from the divine, especially in difficult conversations. The truth needs to be heard.

God does not expect us to be perfect, but He does expect us to try. He expects us to listen to one another and put conscious effort into what we are doing, for whom we are doing it, and for what purpose. When we do for others, we inspire others to do the same. We must have respect for one another. We become role models for what is right and just rather than gaining negative momentum. When we choose to react with envy, jealousy, greed, or arrogance, we are choosing evil. And when we fall away from the light, we fall away from God. Difficult questions and difficult conversations can go bad really fast, especially when one person isn't being truthful. Sometimes unfiltered conversations or direct questions are only accepted by people with certain personality types, certain members of the family, or people of the male gender. To others, they can seem too bold. If you want to be truthful, learn it here—on the earthly plane. Once you cross over and meet your creator, you won't be able to fool Him. He is the judge. Great spiritual leaders agree that we are all one, one in the whole of the divine, the Lord, Jesus Christ. It is in grace that we have faith, where our beliefs are then embedded into our soul.

We don't communicate with words when we cross over. Our thoughts will be our words; the communication will be instantaneous. There will be no opportunity to divert the conversation by thinking, *How can I get out of this?* Yes, all souls who cross over are subject to a life review. Sometimes it even happens when people have a near-death experience (NDE), to which I will dedicate a chapter.

Knowing that God exists and trusting our inner voices takes us to another level of spiritual domain. We suffer deeply if we don't trust ourselves. We must be devoted to ourselves before we can devote ourselves to anyone else. Any therapist will tell you that. There needs to be a healthy balance between your physical domain, your emotional domain, and your spiritual domain. When your spirit is in alignment with the divine, you won't question your *intuition*. You not only trust that God exists but also trust yourself. He always speaks to us. Many people do not fully know God because they do not trust themselves to accept that inner voice through which God speaks to them. People often misinterpret phrases in the Bible or make comments that do not accurately reflect what scripture says. God gives us special gifts, and we are to accept and honor these gifts. Do good with your gifts and help others. Be humble with one another. Understand that the ways in which people are taught vary from culture to culture, from religion to religion, as well as from family to family. Our ways may not align with our teachings, yet we all still have something here to learn from one another. Everyone's calling is different, and not honoring your calling goes against the will of God. Just make sure that what you feel you are called to do aligns with the Bible. Only God, our Lord Jesus Christ, provides us with these gifts—He is the one and only source. There is no mistaken identity when God speaks to us. We need to trust that we know Him. Get over the need for approval from someone else; your relationship with God is between you and God only. You must understand that. Don't settle for the status quo. You are a magnificent soul in the eyes of God. You are His divine creation. Don't let Him down. He doesn't make garbage. Trust your gut, and trust yourself. Trust that you are unconditionally loved and cared for, and trust that He is always speaking to you.

Joseph Lumpkin writes in his book *The Lost Books of the Bible: The Great Rejected Texts* (2009),–– "Satan has the power to produce apparitions, specters, and illusions, so believable that they cannot be distinguished from reality. Satan lies and offers material enticements—even these may be confused with the grace of God. After all, God gave Adam treasures to place in the cave for his comfort and consolation." He adds, "Stop. Be Still. Look within. Satan can manipulate the material world but cannot touch the spirit. The soul is the domain of God."

Have humility. We have the tendency to judge situations and people we know nothing about. Only God knows. We are all servants of Christ and heaven—even here on earth we serve heaven. No mortal human is more important than anyone else of any race, sex, culture, or religion. It is through the resurrection of Christ that we enter heaven, but here on earth we do have free will and must encourage one another to do good. You will know God when you see Him, encounter Him, or have a dream of Him—there is no question of who He is when your energy meets and interacts with His. That I know for sure.

There is a grace of courage in faith that sustains your soul through the trials and tribulations of life. When we sacrifice ourselves to the Lord and trust in the journey that He is leading us on, we can then be assured that nothing can harm us. We need to stop the fears, stand up for what is right and just, and above all, not be afraid to speak up.

Let's hear what different Christian ministers had to say on the question of what it means to believe versus having faith.

Father C. George Mary Claret, Roman Catholic priest:

- "Belief is 'knowledge' and faith is 'accepting what God has in store for me.'"
- "In belief, God is revealing Himself to us, but faith is much deeper."
- "Faith is the relationship we have with God."
- "In scripture it says, God loved us so much He gave us His only begotten son."

Reverend Miguel Bustillos, exorcist, and nondenominational Christian minister from Maryland: "Faith is your belief that there is a God without seeing Him or measuring it—it is a spiritual acceptance."

Reverend Joseph Pennella, Catholic-raised evangelical, Pentecostal minister from Connecticut: "Faith is much stronger than belief."

Reverend Dr. John H. Krahn, Lutheran minister from Long Island:

- "I believe the terms 'belief' and 'faith' are used interchangeably."
- "One can believe in a higher power, but one who has faith in a higher power is something different."
- "Faith encourages us to make an active difference in our lives."

Baptist reverend Kevin Hartman: "Belief is summarized—it's natural. However, faith is supernatural—it's the hope that there is something greater than yourself."

Interfaith ordained reverend Angela Heil from Long Island, who was originally raised Roman Catholic: "Believing is not always a determination of goodness; it is different than having faith."

TAKING INVENTORY

1. Do you believe in God?
2. Do you have faith and trust in God?
3. Do you understand the difference between belief and faith?
4. How would you define belief versus faith?
5. If someone asked you to speak up for God in a group of people who hate Him, would you stand up for Him?
6. And if you did stand up for Him, just how meaningful would that be?
7. *That is the ultimate trial of faith, and it will happen.*

Two

GOOD DEEDS ARE A TESTIMONY TO FAITH

Be careful therefore, to do as the Lord, your God, has commanded you,
not turning aside to the right or to the left, but following exactly the
way prescribed for you by the Lord, your God, that you may live and
prosper, and may have long life in the land which you are to occupy.
— Deuteronomy 5:32–33

What are good deeds? Good deeds are the things we do out of the kindness
of our own hearts. Doing them results in goodwill because the *intention*
behind them comes from pure sincerity—they are not motivated by a
personal or political gain. Like Gary Zukav wrote in his book *The Seat of
the Soul,* "Every action, thought, and feeling is motivated by an intention,
and that intention is a cause that exists as one with an effect." To further
clarify that, if you agree to assist in a cause such as racism awareness and
your motivation is to do so to gain political notoriety, not because you
are genuinely concerned, that will change the effect or the outcome. If
your *intention* is not divinely good, the outcome will also not be divinely
good. Whatever we do needs to be of pure intention; otherwise, we risk

dissipating the flow of that potentially good energy or causing it to become negative energy. The cause may be good, but if the *intention* is not good, then the outcome will most likely not be good either. Every intention is aligned first with our thoughts.

Pope Benedict, in his book *What Is Christianity?* states, "A saint is a person open to God, permeated by God—someone who does not focus his attention on himself, but makes us see and recognize God." This sums up my point in a nutshell. He goes on to say, "God's healing goodness becomes visible in a way that surpasses human abilities." And this leads me to my next point.

God gives all of us unique gifts—what we do with those gifts is up to us. It could be as simple as smiling, listening to someone as they express their thoughts or concerns, helping someone carry their groceries to the car, volunteering, or working in public service as a police officer, nurse, doctor, teacher, or rescue worker and doing that mission with honesty and integrity. The list can go on and on. The point is that no matter what else we do in our daily lives, we can do good deeds that serve God. Joy is a state of grace in which, no matter what is going on around you, you are in bliss because of faith in God. So remember that your unique gifts are your special ways in which you can serve God. When we are not on the right path in life, we feel it and know it. Don't let pride or arrogance feed into the desire to do something other than what you're meant to do. Anything that serves God in a positive light and brings positive healing energy to others demonstrates goodness, kindness, hope, and joy.

> The King will reply, "Truly I tell you, whatever you did
> for one of the least of these brothers and sisters of mine,
> you did for me." (Matthew 25:42)

If you don't know what your purpose is, what your unique gifts and talents are, discover that first. Many self-help books on the market today can help. In fact, my first book provided worksheets designed to help others discover their purpose. As a recreational therapist, I ran three to four groups a day mentoring mentally ill and physically disabled people discover what their abilities were. We are not all meant to be rocket scientists. God created us to be unique, and one gift is not any better than another—it's just different. Don't walk through life thinking, *I'm not good enough* or *I'm not this or that.* You are exactly as you're meant to be. Don't throw it away and don't doubt yourself. Listen inwardly—listen to that inner voice. Whatever you do, make it positive.

The text of 1 Thessalonians chapters 2 and 3 talks about mutual charity, not depending upon anyone, minding our own affairs, working with our own hands, and conducting ourselves properly with outsiders. Jesus states, "If a man is not willing to work, he shall not eat." What does that mean? It means that we do not go to heaven for our works, but our works demonstrate our faith. This is important in understanding that good deeds do matter because they are our testimony to our faith.

As a recreational therapist I worked with many people with diverse disabilities, as well as in diverse health-care settings. Each institution had a similar yet unique mission to operate with honesty, integrity, responsibility, kindness, and compassion. Quality management departments within the institutions oversee the services provided, including the integrity involved in ensuring best practices. I also worked for Stony Brook Medicine in their Continuous Quality Improvement Department, assisting with internal audits on government regulations and certifiers to provide oversight on various medical units of the hospital in which data is collected for quality assurance projects. Oversight is an important part of the health-care industry. Governing bodies have ethical committees and subcommittees to ensure best practices not only in health care but in other kinds of corporations as well. In our own lives, we need to monitor our ethics, honesty, and integrity in the practice of life. It's no different. In every institution, religion, and governing body, there is a time when policies, laws, or regulations appear unjust, immoral, and inhumane. Stand up for what is not right or accurate. If policies are not working or are not being adhered to, speak up. Use your voice. Assert yourself with courage, and God will be with you as you do— no matter to whom you are speaking. Remember, Jesus is your boss, and God is your boss; everyone else is just playing a role in your life. This is the earth school. We are here to learn to live according to God's plan. There's no room for error in heaven. It must be learned here.

In the ministry of Christ, do not neglect the gift you were given. Remember, we too can generate grace toward one another through our work, our patience, our kind acts, our generosity, our wisdom, and our voices.

In my personal opinion, if good deeds were enough, we would have no need for Christ to come to earth. Good deeds are not all that matter—they are only the tip of the iceberg. The Bible says, "You are saved by grace through faith in Christ Jesus and not by our own efforts or work" (Ephesians 2:8–9).

Let's hear what the Christian ministers say from personal interviews with me on the topic of good deeds and if they ultimately do matter.

Father Claret:

- "Yes, good deeds do matter and so does our faith—both matter."
- "We are accountable for our 'being' and 'doing.' Our relationship is our 'being' with Him; and our 'doing' is our 'union' with Him—understanding that Jesus Christ is living in 'me.'"

Reverend Bustillos:

- "Faith without works is dead, so yes, good deeds do matter."
- "Without Christ we will all fail."

Reverend Joseph Pennella: "Jesus said, I am the way, the truth, and the life. No one comes to the father except through me."

Reverend Boggs: "According to the Bible and teachings of the early church, it takes both faith and good deeds to go to heaven; the good deeds are the result of our faith and a natural response to our love for God and our fellow human beings."

Reverend Krahn:

- "Faith encourages an active difference in your life."
- "As Christians we are called to make an active difference in a positive way—we go to church to praise God, to worship God, and to ultimately thank God, and since we are born into sin, all sin strays us from God."
- "As a Christian of faith, we are called to love, to forgive, and to be involved because of our faith."

Revered Hartman:

- "Yes, it does take more than good deeds to get to heaven."
- "By grace we are saved in our faith, but it is important to uphold righteousness."
- "You must bear the fruit—your works are a byproduct of you being saved."

Revered Heil:

- "It does take more than good deeds to go to heaven; it takes kindness, sincerity."
- "It's not just the doing; it is the intention."
- "You must balance the good versus evil—kindness is more important than anything else."

TAKING INVENTORY

1. Do you believe that good deeds matter in your effort to get to heaven?
2. Do you believe Jesus's dying on the cross grants you permission to sin as much as you want? Think about that.
3. What good deeds have you done in your life?
4. Do you believe that good deeds make up for our sins?
5. Last, do you believe that your faith requires you to do good deeds?

Three

WHY AM I HERE?

> All good giving and every perfect gift is from above,
> coming down from the Father of lights, with whom
> there is no alteration or shadow caused by change.
> — James 1:17

We all have divine gifts given to us by God. We are each here for a divine purpose, also called our sacred contract. If you haven't ever read Caroline Myss's book *Sacred Contracts*, I recommend it. Our sacred contracts are our personal core lessons that we need to accomplish on this earth while we are here. We all need to learn basic life lessons, and our sacred contracts are our individual core lessons. If you have ever read or listened to stories of NDEs, you have heard people talk about being sent back, or not dying, because they had yet to accomplish their sacred contracts. That is exactly why some people don't die.

I once had a dream that I had accomplished most of my goals and all of my primary goals in life. Disgusted with the way the world is, I had a conversation with God in my head. I told him I was ready to go. In my dream, I was in the middle of the ocean with my sisters and mother with no land in sight, and a ladder suddenly fell out of the sky. I said to my mother and sisters, "Come on, I want to go up the ladder. Let's go." They said, "No way! We don't want to go there yet." I looked at them so completely puzzled. I knew they were Catholic and that they believed in God. *What is their problem?* I thought. I felt so disgusted with them. The ladder that had appeared was a rope ladder, sort of like one you would see on a boat or as a fire escape from a window. I climbed up the ladder, and when I got to the top, I found a hatch, just like one on the roof of a cabin inside a boat. I knocked on the hatch and yelled, "Let me in! I'm ready to enter heaven." Two angels opened the hatch and smiled ever so gently; they looked at each other. I said, "Please let me in. I'm done with earth." They gently chuckled and said, "Well, we could let you in, but you haven't finished all of your life lessons yet, and that means you would have to go back." I felt myself get all flustered; I was so let down. I said, "What do you mean—I would have to be reborn?" They said, "Yes." I quickly descended the ladder and jumped into the ocean water, and my mother and sisters said, "What happened?" I said, "They told me I'd have to come back to this place and be reborn—and there's no way I'm coming here again!" My mother and my sisters burst out laughing in my dream. In fact, they cracked up when I told them about my dream in real life too. It is a funny story—and I could see it happening. I'm not encouraging the idea of reincarnation—I really don't think we have the answers to that—but what I know for sure is that we must concentrate on this day and this hour. And that's enough to handle.

The point of this story is that I feel with all my heart and soul that it was a message given to me by God. It was an epiphany of clarification that we don't just check out when we want to—and if we do, there are consequences. We do have free will, and our free will is sometimes not in our hands. For example, some people are murdered, and accidents happen that claim someone's life before what we perceive as their time. The truth of the matter is that there is much more going on as far as our fate goes than we truly understand. Of course, I don't believe it is written in the book, or predestined, for someone to be murdered or even die in a car accident. What I do know is that those who have returned from an NDE have stated that there are windows through which one can pass. If an accident happens before that time frame, all of heaven stops it from claiming the person's life. This is why we see miracles happen with no explanation. God is always watching—always.

In Pat Longo's book *The Gifts Behind Your Anxiety,* Longo states, "We are spiritual beings, having a human experience." Each of us, she reiterates, "has spiritual gifts to recognize, protect, and develop for our own greater good." Our intuition is a sensing outside of our five senses, and that manifests to more spiritual gifts. Trust your intuition. Empaths are people who have heightened sensitivity to other emotions; they are energy sponges. They feel the emotions of people, groups, and animals more intensely than others, and those emotions cause anxiety.

You have to remember that we are all divinely connected through God's light. God is in us; we are His children, His creation. Through divine *free will,* we have the ability to make our own choices as God granted us—and yes, we do have to be mindful of the choices we make. All choices begin with a thought. Thoughts can be good or bad, and we set our intentions with thoughts. As Longo stated in her book, "Thoughts are the difference between fear and faith; and also, between prison and freedom." We must be careful how we consciously set our intentions through thought because thoughts are used to influence our own energy and the energy that exists around us. We must make sure they align with scripture and God. To provide more clarity on this topic in scientific or medical terms, the energy of the body through thought gains power and expands through the mental body into the emotional body, and we produce a feeling (such as fear and anxiety). If we continue to hold onto this feeling, it can move into our physical bodies in the form of a stomachache or nausea.

To provide more insight in regard to NDEs, not all of us are meant to grow old. This is why some children pass away. We don't all need to live full lifetimes. This is where faith and trust fall into place. If you know God, you know we don't ever truly die. We only leave this place called earth. There is no death; our lesson on earth is just over. School is out. However, living with grief is very difficult for those who have lost loved ones. The only thing that gets us through that is faith. Trust in God, believing He is in charge and knowing that He is always with us, watching us, and protecting us.

If you don't know what your purpose is, there are tools you can use, such as a leisure inventory checklist or interest sheet, to discover your passions. As a health-care practitioner, I would use many of these tools with my clients to help them overcome depression and anxiety. Some people may not know what career path to choose, and others are held back by life's troubles. You are not alone, and there are many self-help and self-discovering mechanisms to choose from. If you are stumbling while searching for a career path, there are hundreds of possibilities, more than ever before. Technology has advanced so much that many things for which you may have a passion are accessible online. Some people are passionate for teaching, preaching, politics, writing, poetry, holistic wellness, medicine, science, math, or creative arts—including singing, painting, creating abstract art, playing instruments, engaging in theater or the performing arts. For some it's recording music; for others it's construction and building. Remember, Rome wasn't built in a day. Many team-building projects and visions have changed the world in a positive way, and we have many remarkable advancements in medicine and medical technology. The point is that opportunity in this world is endless. We are all driven by the lifeforce energy within us, given to us by God, our spirits, our souls, and our lust for life. That is our purpose. Your unique gift to the world is to make it better than it was before your time. Do what you love and bring love and joy to others in your inspirations and aspirations. Always speak positively toward others regarding your goals because, when you do, you bring inspiration and positive energy back to them.

The way you carry out your life's purpose is ultimately determined by you, but whatever path you choose, make sure it is aligned with Christ's teachings. In any career path or any relationship we choose, we need to be aware of negative influences so we can confront them. Be mindful to react in a way that is aligned with God.

Let's see what the Christian ministers have to say regarding our purpose and why we are here on earth.

Father Claret:

- "Our purpose is to be made in the likeness of Christ."
- "We are to be transformed into the likeness of Jesus as stated in scripture."

Reverend Bustillos:

- "Our purpose is to serve God."
- "But if God is not present, then it should be whatever motivates you to continue living."

Reverend Pennella:

- "We are here to fulfill God's purpose for us."
- "We are here to learn not to be selfish, to fulfill God's will by serving one another."

Reverend Krahn:

- "Our purpose is to make an active difference in a positive way."
- "Faith calls us to have an active difference in the struggles of our lives."

Reverend Hartman:

- "We in a sense give our life to God—to serve."
- "We must listen to God's voice—the one you have been called to."
- Reverend Hartman quoted Jeremiah 1:5: "Before I formed you in the womb I knew you."

Reverend Boggs:

- "The purpose of life is to become deified god beings."
- "'God became man, so that man might become God,' as stated by St. Athanasius."
- "The purpose of our life is to become deified humans, the same as Christ Jesus." "We will not become like God in essence, but like Him in how we love."

Reverend Heil: "We are here to learn to be kind; kindness more than anything else."

TAKING INVENTORY

1. Do you know why you are here on this earth?
2. What is your purpose?
3. Do you believe your purpose changes?
4. Do you believe you have a major and a minor purpose?
5. What are your gifts?
6. Do you give glory to others?
7. Do you inspire others?
8. Do you speak in a positive light of your passions to yourself and to others?
9. What do you feel you were put on earth to do?
10. Does your purpose give glory to God?

Four

VARIOUS KINDS OF SINS

Therefore, I say to you, every sin and blasphemy will be forgiven
people, but blasphemy against the Spirit will not be forgiven.
— Matthew 12:31

What is sin? Sin is an immoral act considered to be a transgression against
divine law—a sin in the eyes of God (Oxford Dictionary).

> For if we live, we live to the Lord, and, if we die, we die
> to the Lord. So then, whether we live or whether we die,
> we are the Lord's. (Romans 14:8)

The Bible talks about many kinds of sins, but there is one sin that is
unforgiveable and that is blasphemy of the Holy Spirit. This is the refusal
to acknowledge the presence of God in Christ prior to your physical death
or before the Second Coming of Christ. The only way to heaven is through
Christ. There is no other way. Not all religions follow this, and not all
religions believe in Jesus Christ as the son of God, born in the flesh as the

Messiah. If they don't know it now, they will know it at death, and they will certainly know it at the end of time.

The book of Revelation speaks of the end of times and what signs to look for. There will be an illumination of consciousness and awakening prior to the miracle, as the Blessed Mother told Conchita Gonzalez in a small village in Garabandal of Northern Spain—one of the four children during the apparitions of the Blessed Mother there in the years 1961–1965. Conchita is still alive today, and she claims the illumination of consciousness is to occur soon. At that time, all souls on the earth will learn and be fully aware that Jesus Christ is the Messiah, the son of God. People will have no question as to who Christ is—the time then will be close to the Second Coming of Christ's return to the earth. This earth age will then end, and a new, third earth age will begin. Not all Christian religions follow this belief. There are many interpretations of the end of times and what that means, which will be in the commentary at the end of this chapter.

According to Gonzalez, within one year of the illumination of consciousness, a *miracle* will occur in the same village in Spain where the apparitions appeared in the early 1960s. This miracle or sign will be illuminated across the globe, seen everywhere until the last day—when the Lord returns. You can read more about this miracle and the illumination of consciousness in Xavier Reyes-Ayral's book *Revelations: The Hidden Secret Messages and Prophecies of the Blessed Virgin Mary*. The book contains significant information that will be valuable for the end times.

Other miracles and apparitions have taken place, some even earlier. In 1917, three shepherd children at Cova da Iria in Fatima, Portugal—Lucia dos Santos and Francisco and Jacinta Marto—had visions of the Blessed Mother. Sister Lucia published memoirs of two secrets revealed to her from the Virgin Mary; the third was revealed to the Catholic church in 1960. You can listen to updates regarding these messages on YouTube, as well as in many published books regarding these apparitions and miracles that happen there. The secrets that were revealed foretold future events that would occur, including wars, natural disasters, and events. Some of these events have already happened as revealed; others are prophesized to happen soon. Hundreds of thousands of people still make pilgrimages to Fatima to witness miracles in the sky and to see this holy place. These messages are pleas from the Blessed Mother to pray because the sins of the world are worse now than ever in history. God will not allow evil to continue, and many people, many of God's children, will be condemned to hell for eternity if they don't turn back to Christ. Freedom of choice is temporary. We must live by God's law to be saved. Evil cannot prevail and won't prevail. God will return, and He will be returning soon.

The seven deadly sins are not listed in the Bible but are consistent with what are called capital vices or cardinal sins. They are pride, greed, wrath, envy, lust, gluttony, and sloth. These sins are often depicted in paintings, sculptures, and statues in museums and churches around the world, as well as at the Vatican.

Let me get into the origin of sin, how this all leads to Jesus's Second Coming, and the different Christian beliefs regarding sin. Original sin is Christian doctrine that, through the fact of birth, we inherit sin because of the sin of Adam and Eve, who were the first humans to be born in the state of sinfulness. Augustine of Hippo, who lived in AD 354–430, coined the term *original sin*. Sin, however, existed before Adam and Eve in the first earth age in the book of Genesis, when the Nephilim were alive. Much of the early books of the Bible were removed, including the book of Enoch, which provides more insight regarding what happened in those early ages.

The *first earth age* occurred during the time of the dinosaurs and was the time when Satan was cast out of heaven, along with the fallen angels. Some say the Nephilim were the fallen angels. According to the Bible study website, the first earth age was also a time when all souls were created—it was our spiritual life. The Jewish commentary on the Torah states that the Talmud essentially says "that in heaven there is a *guf,* a place where souls are waiting to be born, and the Messiah will not be born until all those souls have been born." According to Bible studies, the *gap theory* asserts that the time that lapsed from Genesis 1:1 to Genesis 1:2 was enormously long. This information is often referenced in the Shepherd's Chapel. That would explain why the ancient pyramids were formed so perfectly—they were built in a time when we had no physical bodies. We existed only in spirit and moved things using our conscious energy.

Original sin is thought to have been present at the time when the first two humans were created, Adam and Eve, because of their sin in the Garden of Eden—not listening to God and eating the forbidden fruit.

According to the first earth age movement, there was sin before Adam and Eve, so original sin did not with the sin of Adam. You will hear more insight on this topic from my personal interviews with various ministers of different Christian faiths.

Caroline Myss states in her book *Intimate Conversations with the Divine*, "Divine love is the grace you need in order to heal the wounds in your heart that you cannot heal yourself" and "our conscience alerts us to what is right or wrong." We suffer because of our own sins, and we suffer because of sins of humanity.

The sins of humanity go to great degrees of disobedience—from common white lies, gossip, jealousy, and envy to deceit and varying degrees of criminal activity. It is important to note that no one person starts off with the worst of sins; these sins start off subtle or sublime, not seemingly offensive or inhumane. But people do commit horrific crimes that can blind the eyes of those closest to them. In the next few chapters I will get into more detail of these very specific behaviors that lead to the most horrendous acts and down a very dark path.

St. Augustine in his book *Confessions* described crimes as "committed when emotions turn to actions, and when these actions are corrupt, one revolts and losses control." He goes on to state that sins are acts of self-indulgence and are committed when the *soul* fails to govern the bodily impulses, which thereby are derived by pleasure."

Intention is the reason for which a sin may occur, and it *does* matter. I don't just think this; I know this. We do have a life review, as we have heard in testimony of millions of NDEs across the world in books, podcasts, interviews with physicians, journalists, and so on. This is not a topic people would lie about, and if they did, I don't think a million-plus people would continue to lie about the same thing. All their stories are very similar, and most said they had a partial or full life review. Many were quite lucky to have had this experience as it changed their lives dramatically for the better. All people who have had NDEs say that what we do, what we say, and what we think all matters. Some sins are so horrific, outrageous, and dreadfully evil that they're unimaginable. These include abortion, torture, sex trafficking, rape, murder, emotional and physical abuse, as well as sexual abuse of any kind. Just as there are levels of sin, there are levels of hell and heaven, and each is commensurate to the life lived.

When we pray—especially when we pray for the grace of seeing clearly any dark forces—we will receive God's protection. We have free will; we have the choice to not accept God or Jesus Christ; but when we stray from the Lord, we are more susceptible to the devil. The devil is real, and there are demons. If there were not, then the world would be a perfect place and it's not. So pray for the grace of protection through the blood of Jesus Christ to not be led into temptation of any evils. Pray the Rosary. I have found the Rosary to be the holiest of prayers, so much so that I can see the divine light within me. I am not the only one to have experienced this phenomenon. I will provide a Rosary prayer for you at the end of this book.

Getting back to suffering, the most incomprehensible suffering is that of victims of child sex trafficking and torture of any kind. Even in the midst of the darkest act, there is a God, and heaven is bearing witness. We know that God will not allow evil to win. Free will allows people to do bad but not without consequences, and the consequence of sin is eternity in hell. Scripture includes much that testifies to that for a very good reason. God does not want anyone to go to hell, but sin of great magnitude will not be forgiven if repeated over and over with no remorse. Grace is not a blissful wonder; it is God's mercy on us. Through Jesus Christ's resurrection on the cross, He died for all sins of humanity. But He never said we aren't accountable for the sins we personally commit.

Coming from Catholic faith, I know the Catholic church declares that, through baptism, original sin is erased by imparting the life of Christ's grace. It erases original sin and turns humans back toward God. According to Roman Catholics, venial sins are those that do not entail damnation of the soul. These may include gossiping, lying, being prideful, coveting, envying, and neglecting to pray or to read the Bible regularly.

According to the Catholic church, mortal sins or cardinal sins are far more serious. These include lust, gluttony, greed, sloth (laziness), anger, envy, and pride. Some of the sins are listed for both venial and mortal sins, but the severity of the sin is far different.

In my *personal* reflections, I have found that these sins have many variables that determine how severe they are. Most of them boil down to *intention*, which I have discussed earlier. I love the quote from Gary Zukav's book *The Seat of the Soul*—I highly recommend this book if you haven't read it. Zukav states, "Every action, thought and feeling is motivated by an intention and that intention is a cause that exists as one with an effect." St. Augustine states in his journaling to God, "Many of the things we do may therefore seem wrong to men but are approved in the light of your knowledge, and many men which applaud this are condemned in your eyes." Both of these statements hold true in the fact that *intention* is the pivotal context by which sins are committed—not only due to its cause and effect but by the sheer divine infinite wisdom of God, our Lord and Creator, the only one who truly knows the outcome and consequences for years to come. As humans we cannot comprehend or even imagine the consequence of each cause and effect to one single intention, but the Lord can. When people feel something is justified because "that person deserved it," they don't realize or foresee the aftermath of its destruction for years to come. One action not only *may* be but *will* be "inevitably and ultimately" our ultimate destruction —the onset of WWIII and the Battle of Armageddon.

Let's see what the different Christian minister perspectives are on the topic of sin, including what original sin means, sins of humanity, and the unforgivable sin.

Father Claret:

- There are three kinds of sin: venial sins, capital sins, and mortal sins. "Venial sins are small sins.... Capital sins are the root cause of all sin but involve no action.... Mortal sins are major sins when action is taken."
- "Sins are not determined by law or necessarily perspective law.... The mortal sin, for example, of abortion is legal in some states and countries but will send you to hell if not confessed."
- "The unforgivable sin is blasphemy of the Holy Spirit, which is the rejecting of Jesus and his salvation."
- "Jesus's death and resurrection does wash away original sin, but we still have the inclination to sin—therefore, to be saved, we are still accountable for our sins."

Reverend Bustillos:

- "Original sin started with Adam and Eve."
- "Jesus's death and resurrection still holds us accountable."
- "In Romans, under law we are dead to sin once we accept the Lord Jesus Christ." "Confession of sins is necessary and unless we accept Jesus Christ as our Lord and Savior, demons have legal rights to your soul."
- "Sin is sin, and if you break one sin—you break all."
- "We must ask for forgiveness and have repentance."

Reverend Pennella:

- "Blasphemy of the Holy Spirit is the only unforgivable sin, and that means denying Jesus Christ upon your death."
- He believes in the six-day creation and original sin stemming from the sins of Adam and Eve.
- He believes the sins of humanity are from making choices that don't align with Christ and do need repentance.

Reverend Krahn:

- "It's in sin that my mother conceived me."
- "We are born sinful, and through Jesus Christ's resurrection on the cross we are forgiven; but to be forgiven we must recognize our sins."
- "All sin that is not confessed is straying you from God, and not allow you to enter heaven if not confessed."
- "The unforgivable sin is the sin against the Holy Spirit—denying God."

Reverend Hartman:

- "Original sin is the sin of Adam and Eve."
- "In the Baptist church there are different views, but all uphold the Father, Son, and the Holy Spirit."

- "The unforgivable sin is that of the blasphemy of the Holy Spirit."
- "One can be redeemed, but if a person is so far gone away from Christ, where there is evil—it would take a miracle."

Reverend Heil:

- "As with all sins, there is a cause and effect."
- "For example, killing is not equal to murder. Killing is a necessity at times for survival. There is a purpose such as in wartime or for killing animals to eat, but murder is in your control."
- "Any sin where the innocent are abused would be a mortal sin."

Reverend Boggs:

- "Original sin is a doctrine of the Western church and not believed or shared by Eastern Orthodoxy."
- "We did not inherit the sin of Adam and Eve, but only the consequences of their sin, i.e., death and sickness, as well as a perceived separation from God."
- "To sin is to miss the mark. All human beings do this, but the misunderstanding is that we are separated from God because of our sin. This is erroneous. We are never separated from God. We only believe we are due to false understanding which was created and taught by man-made religions."
- "Jesus came to show us the truth of our divine nature and eventually return home to God."
- "Unforgivable sins is blaspheming the Holy Spirit. It is the only unforgivable sin in the Bible, which is to deny our divine nature. All other so-called sins are forgivable, but truly they are opportunities for spiritual growth and do not separate us from God."

TAKING INVENTORY

1. Do you understand the different kinds of sins?
2. Do you understand the unforgivable sin?
3. Do you believe religion helps guide governments' laws on mortal sin?
4. In your opinion, is society doing a good job of combating evil sins?
5. What needs improvement for society to live according to Christ's teachings?
6. Do you think you can make a difference in a sinful world?
7. What can you commit yourself to doing to improve the world?

Five

WHAT DO REMORSE AND FORGIVENESS MEAN?

Not everyone who says to me, "Lord, Lord," will enter the kingdom
of heaven, but the one who does the will of my Father who is in
heaven. Many will say to me on that day, "Lord, Lord, did we not
prophecy in your name? Did we not drive out demons in your name?
Did we not do mighty deeds in your name?" Then I will declare to
them solemnly, "I never knew you. Depart from me, you evildoers."
— Matthew 7:21–23

God died on the cross for our sins—this is true. Whoever confesses this
is to be forgiven—also true. But are all confessions sincere? Be mindful
of what a confession is and what it means to you. This is not to say that
you shouldn't forgive but rather to ask, "Are your confessions truthful?"

According to Wikipedia, forgiveness is the intentional and voluntary
process by which one who may initially feel victimized or wronged, goes
through a change in feelings and attitude regarding a given offender, and
overcomes the impact of the offense including negative emotions such
as resentment and a desire for vengeance. *Wikipedia* also states that "the

term forgiveness can be used interchangeably and is interpreted many different ways by people and cultures," particularly when it comes to communication. In the Bible, the Greek word for *forgiveness* translates to "let it go"—meaning there is no debt to be paid. According to Bible studies, there are four types of forgiveness—unconditional forgiveness (the highest type of forgiveness we can offer someone who has wronged us), conditional forgiveness, dismissive forgiveness, and grace (forgiveness by God.)

The Bible talks about five steps of true forgiveness: *responsibility, regret, repentance, reconciliation,* and *restitution.* The person must acknowledge the anger and hurt caused by the specific offense. The victim must avoid taking revenge on the other person, consider the offender's perspective, be careful not to transfer the wrongdoing elsewhere, and release it. Reconciliation can happen only if forgiveness has happened. In other words, you cannot heal a relationship if the offender has not recognized what he or she has done wrong. Another important point to remember is that forgiving is not pardoning; you cannot pardon a harmful act. That is never OK. You can be pardoned in a court for a traffic offense; however, when it comes to victimizing another person, it is never just OK. You must learn from the offense. Forgiving is not forgetting either—offenders must always remember the hurt they have caused and be mindful of what the victims have endured to avoid making themselves vulnerable again. God did not put us on this earth to take abuse, under any circumstances. The offenders must feel remorse for them to be granted forgiveness. Taking responsibility for your actions is very important to your soul, and allowing someone to victimize you is not OK. Many vulnerable people are victimized, but once you identify that—once you know or recognize it—it is your responsibility to not let it happen again. Many offenders can and will do it to someone else. The cycle of abuse continues until it is *stopped*!

According to Isaac Newton's law of motion, what goes up must come down. Remember, we are not responsible for the hurtful things that others do; however, we are responsible for how we react. How we react to things causes karma—or in Christian understanding, sin. Reclaim your power by learning and growing from others and teach others the challenges that you've endured to help them. Choose to heal. Holding onto hurt hurts you and can punish you more. Take your life back, in reverence to God.

Don't let toxic energy consume you to be like the person who sinned against you. Release the negative energy or you will transfer that sin and that negative energy onto someone else. And that is exactly what the devil will want you to do.

In what ways can you help yourself? Meditate and pray. Eat healthy, exercise, enjoy nature, and take long walks to breathe in the fresh air God gave us to enjoy on this planet. Appreciate nature and focus on what you do have and all the good in your life God has provided for you. Let go of what you don't have—and trust that God has you right where He wants you. Write in a journal; find a creative talent you may have such as arts and crafts, painting, playing an instrument, or singing; take up a new sport; or find a new friend who is aligned with the same core values and morals as you—in Christ. Whatever outlet you choose, make it a positive choice.

In the next chapter I'm going to talk about liars and manipulation, how those play out in a confession, and the consequence of not really being sorry? This is something to contemplate because we do see it all the time in the workplace, in family life, and with our friends and companions. Do you really mean it when you say you're sorry? Is it an act of kindness, a means to get what you want, or a true expression of remorse? Be the judge of yourself. God will be your second and final judge upon your death in your life review. Remember that when we cross over, we will go through a life review, and it will be in significant detail. From what people who have had NDEs claim, that life review happens in slow motion so that we grasp every sense of not only what we lived but also how others interacted with and reacted to our presence. We will feel everything they felt and more in this life review. We may fool ourselves and others here, but we will never be able to fool God.

Let's see what the different Christian ministers had to say in personal interviews on the topic of remorse and forgiveness.

Father Claret:

- "The degree of the sin has to do with the more you move away from Christ."
- "For there to be forgiveness we must have the condition to repent, and the understanding not to do it again."

- "There is not only no forgiveness without remorse—but there is no forgiveness if you don't have the intention to not do it again."
- "Through the sacrament of reconciliation—a confession that is heard through an ordained priest—forgiveness of the sin happens with the confessed sin; but it is God who forgives."

Reverend Bustillos: "You must have remorse when asking for forgiveness."

Reverend Pennella:

- "You must have remorse to be forgiven."
- "At the end of one's life if they choose to call out to Christ, he will forgive them."
- "God doesn't want the sinner to go to hell—God has much mercy and provides many chances."

Reverend Boggs:

- "There is no forgiveness without remorse."
- "A person must feel remorse in order to be forgiven."
- "It doesn't mean we can't commit the sin again—because we often do repeat our sins over and over again because we are weak."
- "It takes a great deal of time and grace of the Holy Spirit."
- "We have great difficulty overcoming our passions, which is a term used by the Orthodox Church."

Reverend Krahn:

- "The Lutheran church has a general confession of faith and remorse, but it is not mandated to participate."
- "To be forgiven, one must recognize the sin—one must expect remorse."
- He commented that people are generally considered weak, so sins are repeated; but he reiterated that remorse needs to be present.
- He mentioned that in the Lutheran version of the Bible, "We are called to a higher standard to elevate a person when one is in sin ... meaning we cannot engage in gossip or speak unkindly especially publicly regarding one's sin, but rather make an attempt to help that person."

Reverend Hartman:

- "There does have to be remorse for there to be forgiveness—otherwise it is not sincere."
- "However, having remorse does not mean you cannot do it again—to be forgiven." "It goes back to the idea that when we ask for forgiveness of our sins, we need to be remorseful—as humans we do repeat sin."
- "In the Baptist ministry, it is not required to confess to a minister—you can confess to another person or God. Only God can provide the forgiveness of the sin."

Reverend Heil: "When asking for forgiveness there must be remorse for the sin. Having remorse doesn't mean you cannot commit the sin again, but if there was no remorse at all karma will hit when they least expect it."

TAKING INVENTORY

1. Do you see how remorse is important for there to be forgiveness?
2. In your own personal reflections, when you say, "I'm sorry," are you truly remorseful?
3. Do you believe forgiveness is important in your personal life?
4. When you apologize to someone, do you truly mean it? Or do you say it just to make peace?
5. When you ask God for forgiveness, do you truly mean it or just do it to be at peace with yourself?
6. To whom are you most comfortable making a confession?
7. What do you think are the consequences for an insincere apology?
8. Have you ever apologized at all? If not, why not? This is something to think more deeply about. In most arguments, both parties are at fault, but how sincere you are about how the resolution will reflect the outcome. The same holds true of your confessions to Christ.
9. What positive outlets can you use in the future to help you gain insight into your relationships, career choices, or personal encounters with conflicting morals that lead to sin?
10. How can you improve?

Six

PREDATORS

The Most Horrific Crimes—Child Sex Trafficking, Torture, Murder/Abortion

> Then I saw another beast come up out of the earth; it had two horns
> like a lamb's but spoke like a dragon. It wielded all the authority
> of the first beast in its sight and made the earth and its inhabitants
> worship the first beast, whose mortal wound had been healed.
> Revelation 13:11–12

The Bible is explicitly clear on what happens after the Second Coming of Christ in our final judgment. The signs of the end of time are here. The Euphrates River has dried up, we've just gone through the worst epidemic of the century, Christians are being persecuted, there is lawlessness and recklessness in the streets of our cities all over the world, there have been wars and rumors of wars, there have been more and more natural disasters, and the storms are coming in stronger like birth pains, as described in the Bible. The most important sign that we've been told to look out for is the teaching of the Bible all over the world. With the internet available everywhere now, all countries and people have heard of Jesus Christ. There isn't a culture that hasn't heard of Him.

People are very different than they were years ago. There is no respect for proper values and morals. There's no respect for parents, the elderly, teachers, police, physicians, religious leaders, and so on. Many churches are closing because people are no longer going and they are not getting enough funding. People are turning against God, and the Satanic cult is rising. Satanic clubs are now allowed in public schools. Who knew that would ever be allowed? It's sickening to think about. Years ago, governments were aligned with the laws of God—this is no longer true. Churches and religious leaders are becoming more liberal, defying the laws of God and laws of the past. Greed has grown in the church, and very little has been done to pedophiles within the church; many pedophiles are still just moved to another church instead of being prosecuted. Government as well as church leaders have become very lenient on social groups and promoting agendas that go against Christ's teachings, including LGBTQ+ groups, pedophiliac activity, homosexuality, lawlessness, child abuse, and abortion. These are but a few that do not align with scripture and can lead people away from salvation. The United Sates was a country founded on Christian beliefs and faith. It was never separated from Christ until recent generations. We were always free to choose our faith, as God granted us free will; but the core of our values is Jesus Christ's teachings. We do need to fear God, for if we don't, we may not be saved at the end of our lives. Disbelief in God or in Jesus Christ automatically makes people disciples of the Devil. There is no in-between—this is what people are not understanding. It is only by believing in Jesus Christ as the son of God; living a good life by His laws; and through forgiveness, confession, and reconciliation are we saved.

In my travels to Rome in 2019, tour guides and natives within the city explained their frustrations with the disorder within the Vatican. People claimed they weren't given the truth regarding Pope Benedict's unheard-of retirement from the papacy. According to residents, Pope Benedict was going to expose the financial corruptions of the church, the sexual abuse of nuns and children, and homosexual activity of priests. The Roman people and tour guides said that Pope Benedict wanted to put a stop to this. Much of this rhetoric was dismissed as conspiracy theory or rumors passed on by the media or other people, but these claims seem to keep arising. Only the church leaders know the truth, but the issues and crimes within the church are unspeakable acts. When these things happen, it amounts to a statement that it is okay for all to act in this manner. The church is a mentor, an example of how God's children should act. When that is broken, people become broken. Society's morals breakdown. This is also true of government leadership. When there are scandals within the government and through leadership, it opens the door for more corruptions around the globe.

According to the John Jay Reports and reports from Charter for the Protection of Children and Young People on the BishopAccountability. org website, data recorded from 1950 to 2018 indicated that 7,002 clerics were nonimplausibly and credibly accused of sexually abusing minors. According to reports, 118,184 priests were employed on active duty in those years, and these 7,002 were convicted, 5.9 percent of the total. This included 5,808 priests, 35 bishops, 108 deacons, 47 seminarians, 307 brothers, and 119 religious sisters. Data indicates a total of 20,052 victims, but since twenty-seven Latin Rite Diocese did not release lists or names of the clergy, the real numbers are likely higher. On May 31, 2019, these reports were published by the United States Conference of Bishops (USCCB). This is an alarming number of victims and religious leaders involved.

The Statista website says that there were 133,294 reported rape cases in the United States in 2022, a number that has significantly increased since 1990. The National Sexual Violence Resource Center (**www.nsvrc. org**) reported the following statistics:

- 63 percent of sexual assaults are not reported to police.
- One in five women and one in seventy-one men will be raped at some point in their lives.
- Nearly one in ten women have been raped by an intimate partner in her lifetime.
- 91% of the rape victims are female, 9% are male.
- 8% of the rapes occur while the victim is at work.

- 81% of women and 35% of men report significant PTSD (Post Traumatic Stress Disorder) from rape.
- One in four girls and one in six boys will be sexually abused before they turn 18 years old.
- 12.3% of women were 10 years old or younger the first time they were raped.
- 27.8% of men were 10 years old or younger the first time they were raped.
- 96% of the people who sexually abuse children are male; and 76.8% of the people who sexually abuse children were adults.
- And a staggering 325,000 children are at risk of becoming victims of commercial child sexual exploitation each year (www.nsvrc.org).

If these figures aren't alarming you, there is something wrong!

People need to be God fearing. We must remember that sweeping the lies under the carpet doesn't make them go away. In fact, it makes them horribly worse. These kinds of sins are not forgivable without deep remorse and rehabilitation, and even then, is it possible? *I think it would take a miracle.* Consider how these grossly evil acts of sin align with Satan. The seriousness of these horrific crimes, knowing that not all souls will make it to heaven, requires great responsibility on the part of church leaders to set proper morals in society. As a Catholic myself—and I speak of all Christians—if you are a Christian, there is no separation of church and state. Being a Christian requires you to be Christian twenty-four hours a day in every aspect of life. And when you see something wrong, it is your utmost responsibility to say something, especially if an innocent little child is being hurt or exploited in any way. It's disgusting, to say the very least!

Politicians and governments need to stand united to stop crime, including rape and child sex trafficking. Citizens must voice their intolerance for this evil. Women spend far too much time pushing for their right to abortion, while all these rapists are walking away *scot-free.* People don't even seem to get angry at rapists anymore; there's never anything on the news warning women about rapists. It seems to have become old news. Yet women stand outside in the cold weather fighting for the right to choose.

Pope Benedict XVI wrote the book *What Is Christianity?* In chapter 5, he covered the sex scandals in the church, saying, "The extent and gravity of the reported incidents have deeply distressed priests and lay people alike, leading more than a few to call into question the very faith of the Church." He blamed the freedoms of the Revolution of 1968 for society's becoming more sexually overt to the point we no longer have any norms. He felt that even pedophilia was proclaimed as permissible and appropriate. He further added that homosexual cliques were formed that markedly changed the climate in seminaries. At the common meals, seminarians ate together with other lay pastors who were sometimes accompanied by their wives and children or fiancées. Pope Benedict stated, "In a society where God is absent, a society no longer knows him and treats him as if he did not exist, is a society that loses its standards. When God dies in society—we were assured—it becomes free." He said in one of his conversations with a victim of pedophilia, a young woman who was sexually assaulted while serving as an altar server, said the pastor, who was her superior, always introduced the sexual abuse he committed with the words, "This is my body which is given for you." He strongly stated, "We as a society must implore the Lord for forgiveness, and above all else we must beg him and ask him to teach us all to understand again the magnitude of his Passion, of his sacrifice. And we must do all we can to protect the gift of the Holy Eucharist from abuse." He felt that the book of Revelation tells us to manifest. The accusation against God focuses above all on discrediting his church as a whole and thereby turning us away from her. The idea of a better church of our own creation is really a proposal of the Devil, using deceitful logic that we fall for much too easily. The church, Pope Benedict goes on to emphasize, "is not only made up of some bad fish, and she is the instrument by which God saves us. There is sin in the Church and there is evil. But today," he stated in his book, "there is also the Holy Church, which is indestructible."

Abortions are another horrific crime. Life begins in the womb. People today are more willing to save baby animals or insects than they are humans. Today's medical technology is so advanced we know a baby is fully developed by eight weeks, the typical point at which abortions are done. Abortion is murder—there is no question here. There should be no question of that for any Christian. Babies in the womb have a heartbeat at five weeks; they can move, kick, suck their thumbs, hiccup, poop, pass urine, breathe in amniotic fluid, and the list goes on and on. If you are

Christian and even vote for a president, *for example,* who allows abortion, it is a sin. To me this is clearly emphasized in the Bible: *"Thou shall not kill."*

According to the World Health Organization (WHO) in a report on November 25, 2021, six out of ten of all unintended pregnancies end in an induced abortion. Around 45 percent of all abortions are unsafe, of which 97 percent take place in developing countries. An alarming number—73 million—of abortions take place worldwide each year according to the WHO and the Guttmacher Institute. That is an outstanding number of lives lost! Did you know that seven US states and Washington DC have no limits on abortion? Although most abortions occur during the first eight to fifteen weeks of pregnancy, there is still a small percentage of late-term and partial-birth abortions (PBA). This does happen every day according to a September 3, 2023, news article by Jeanne Mancini. This act is grossly sinful. Physicians have explained in detail what actually happens, and the baby does feel it. According to Dr. Anthony Levatino, who posted a video on YouTube, explains using footage of what actually occurs in first-, second-, and third-trimester abortions. The babies are grossly ripped apart with a sopher clamp. This is a tool that has razor-sharp teeth, and once it has a hold of the baby it doesn't let go. The physician then pulls hard, and the baby's limbs are pulled out and mutilated one by one. This tool, Dr. Levatino claims, is used because, after twenty-four weeks of pregnancy, doctors cannot suction out a baby. Many physicians and medical staff have nightmares regarding the procedures they have performed. And make no mistake about it—even in the second trimester, babies feel their limbs being ripped out one by one. Sounds horrible, doesn't it? Have I gotten your attention yet? Do you really think the fetus is not a baby at this point? Why does society feel it's OK to justify this act just because the baby is tiny? No matter what circumstance the mother is going through, this act is outrageously sick! Would a mother throw a two-year-old in a garbage can because the father was abusing her? We all know the answer is no. So why in the world would she torture an innocent baby to death? Why?

In cases of PBA, the abortion physician reported having to dilate the mother's cervix and deliver half of the baby's body out of the womb—either starting from the feet to the naval area or headfirst to the midtorso. Then they kill the baby by crushing its head or suctioning its brain. If this isn't torture, I don't know what is. Now guess what, folks—Jesus Christ said, "Do onto others what you would have them do unto you" (Luke 6:31, Matthew 7:12).

The public needs to take responsibility for these gross acts of mutilation. Constituents who vote for a president or prime minister who supports abortion in a democratic government enable it to occur. They took part in making it a government issue as soon as they voted yes or no. This is part of the problem! Their hands are bloody. They played a part in each baby's death that happened while that elected official was in office if it was legalized. We aren't supposed to judge, but we have every right to make good choices—ethical decisions that keep humans safe.

Abortions are legal in most states, government officials have extended the gestational age for termination of pregnancy, and open borders have enabled child sex trafficking to become completely out of control. It's incredibly dangerous. Laws and regulations are not allowing for proper punishment of these crimes. The deep state is so corrupt that there aren't any trustworthy governmental bodies to handle these kinds of crimes anymore if there ever were. It is so disheartening to recognize the cruel world we live in!

Now let's take a look at what happened in the biggest criminal sex-trafficking case exposed on national television—Epstein Island. Jeffrey Epstein was an elite socialite who was friends with many politicians and celebrities, who visited his island many times. Many popular names were on his visitors list, yet no one mentions or talks about that on national television. It's discussed on YouTube podcasts or on social media, but it is eventually censored to protect the elite. The evil in the world today is beyond what it has ever been in history. Public election campaigns have become political scams, supporting discrimination against people based on class, race, religion, or gender. It's all for political gain. Politicians offer many promises but no solutions, and the juvenile attacks on each party are shamefully embarrassing, especially as a nation that airs its media's boxing-ring campaigns around the world. There is no respect.

Celebrities and Democrats supported riots in the streets to influence political agendas—claiming racism and compassion for the poor—yet when homeless girls were procured by Jeffrey Epstein and Ghislaine Maxwell, there was very little media coverage. Maxwell's trial wasn't aired on national television. Why? There was very little coverage on what

Epstein's friends were doing on the island and what interactions they had with these trafficked girls—one can only assume the worst. The most evil and Satanic act on this planet is child sex trafficking. It has become the fastest-growing international crime network the world has ever seen. Jim Caviezel, an actor in the movie *Sound of Freedom,* did a remarkable job portraying Tim Ballard, the Homeland Security government agent who risked and continues to risk his life rescuing many of these children. In the United States alone, over 350,000 children are identified as missing each year, and at least 100,000 of them are trafficked. That's 30 percent of the missing children. According to *Forbes* magazine, $150 billion are spent each year on trafficking. California and Texas have the highest rates of sex trafficking, which has already surpassed the legal arms trade in terms of money spent and will soon surpass the drug trade. *We have 50 million modern-day slaves in the world today, more than ever before in history, according to the International Labor Organization.* That is appalling!

In addition to child sex trafficking, we are facing the uprising issue of the drug adrenochrome. It is known as an elite drug due to the nature of how it is produced. Some say it is conspiracy theory, but I know people who have worked for big corporations such as Disney and claim they know actors who have taken this drug. Some claim the drug reverses the aging process, at least temporarily. I don't claim this to be true, but in any case, the thought of using a drug that is created by grossly evil acts for any purpose is horrible. A few years back, Ellen DeGeneres made actress Sandra Bullock publicly admit that she had gotten a facial using the fetal tissue of a baby's penis in her skin treatment to reduce aging. This was aired live on her TV show *Ellen.* How outrageous is that? And they both chuckled about it on the show, like there was nothing wrong with it. The world has gone absolutely mad!

For those of you who may not know what adrenochrome is, it is a chemical compound produced by the oxidation of adrenaline—which is only achieved by scaring the daylights out of someone that in turn produces the chemical adrenochrome in their blood. That is then harvested and reproduced for sale and production to Hollywood celebrities and the elite who can afford it. It's also known as a Satanic ritual to receive aborted fetuses' or children's blood in elite clubs. Originally this was considered a conspiracy theory; now it is more often spoken about on podcasts, radio, and YouTube channels. This sin is off the charts as the most disgusting, most horrifying act anyone could do. It involves the torture of children and adults in the modern sex slavery network. Caviezel speaks about this publicly on podcasts to bring an awareness of the evils of Hollywood and elite underground trafficking networks. In God's law it is utterly unforgivable—as we are never to ingest another's blood as a means of pleasure or to ever intentionally harm or hurt another human being for pleasure. It is plain evil. There is only some research on how adrenochrome is produced, but none adds to the ongoing reports that it is used for torture—yet there are numerous stories of this happening.

A research article dated January 22, 2019, and titled "Human Sex Trafficking among Ethiopian Returnees: Its Magnitude and Risk Factors" indicates that the magnitude of human sex trafficking among returning migrants was estimated at 50.89 percent of their population. It was positively associated with the female gender, a strong desire for successful oversea life, a high level of risk-opportunity imbalance before departure, and a strong feeling of hopelessness of success in their home country.

Another research article published on April 19, 2023, "Current Trends in Sex Trafficking Research," indicates that a wide range of definitions of sex-trafficking-related terms is used across different jurisdictions, which leads to a lack of clarity of its impact and impedes detection and prosecution. Research indicates it is a global issue, but there is a lack of information sharing across jurisdictions, which further hinders international prevention and identification efforts. Most research on sex trafficking is done only within the United States, with only some single studies done outside of the United States. Research is limited to minors and does not generally consider risk factors. There is little to no information on special populations such as LGBTQ+ communities that are at high risk. Research also indicates that styles of law enforcement have an impact on the data and more policies need to be set in place for frontline workers to enable early prevention. Data indicates that many vulnerable individuals are the most at risk.

Humans are prone to sin; some are small sins, and others are far more serious. Just remember that Jesus said all sin can be forgiven with confession, asking Him for forgiveness, and reconciliation—making an intention not to do it again. We do repeat sins, and when we have sinned again, we must keep asking for forgiveness. Forgiveness of sins is also two-fold: in order to receive forgiveness, we must also forgive. Don't stray from Jesus, set pure intentions to do better, and learn from your mistakes.

Let's hear what the various Christian ministers had to say in their interviews with me on this topic:

Father Claret:

- "Any physical harm done to another human being is a mortal sin because the sin is taken into action."
- "All are mortal sins; but the degree of the sin does matter because it moves you further and further away from Christ."
- "No sin is unforgivable; however, the sin cannot continue for it to be forgiven and there does absolutely need to be remorse."
- "When we receive forgiveness, we too must forgive others."

Reverend Bustillos:

- "All sin is forgivable."
- "Even the apostle Paul was guilty of mass murders—through his remorse and the forgiveness of Jesus Christ, Paul was forgiven."
- "Although he committed such a horrible crime, keep in mind he still often agonized over having done it—that doesn't always go away."
- "We need to remember it and learn from it."
- "In cases of criminal activities such as child sex trafficking or sexual assault we must prevent the person from doing it again."
- He said that, if someone in his congregation were accused, he would turn them over to the authorities. Even if it was said in a confession, priests are still obligated to prevent further harm to others.

Reverend Pennella:

- "When crimes of such magnitude happen including abortion, torture, murder—it is a double sin."
- "You are not only hurting yourself and God—you are hurting another one of God's children."

Reverend Boggs, responding to a question on the inconceivable crimes of abortion, child sex trafficking, and pedophilia:

- "Abortion is against Orthodox teachings, it is considered a sin equal to murder of an adult human being. The church is a hospital for sick souls, not a courtroom to judge others."
- "All sins can be forgiven in Orthodox teaching and practice, with repentance and a change of life."
- He emphasized that "no sin is forgiven without remorse."
- "You must have remorse and change your life to be like Christ in order to be forgiven."

Reverend Krahn:

- "There are varying levels of sin and opinions in the Lutheran church—ministers do have different opinions on this."
- "In cases of abortion, it is never taken lightly, but in extreme cases where a child was raped or the life of the mother was at stake—makes it challenging."
- Most of his denomination is more open to abortion and supports women's rights. 'Abortion, however, is not an acceptable means of birth control.'
- When he was questioned on the topic of adrenochrome use, he was not aware of what it was.
- "The Lutheran church does see sex trafficking and pedophilia as criminal and as a higher scale of sin."

Reverend Hartman:

- "There's many controversial issues arising out of sin, and one is murder."
- "Some within the Baptist church will agree abortion is murder, while other ministries don't in the exception if a woman's life is threatened or in the instance of rape." Otherwise, "most would agree abortion as a means of birth control is wrong."

- In our discussion of evil, in the realm of inflicting emotional or physical pain onto another, it was clearly emphasized that the Baptist ministries identify it as evil.
- Reverend Hartman claims he had read an article on the use of adrenochrome. He is aware of the evils around the world regarding the use of adrenochrome related to blood harvesting and porn and has even heard of its use in the medical industry. He is also aware of the movie *Sound of Freedom* and says that "what was once considered conspiracy theory appears to be true."
- "From the viewpoint of the Baptist church this is all considered evil."

Reverend Heil:

- "The punishment fits the crime.... There is karma in the world that is equivalent to the action, the cause-and-effect theory.... There is no escaping that." She added, "There is a hell."
- When Reverend Heil was questioned on her knowledge of hurting children for the use of adrenochrome, the known Hollywood drug, she said she hadn't heard of it before.

TAKING INVENTORY

1. How do you feel about evil crimes?
2. What crimes do you consider evil?
3. Who do you define as predators? Think deeply for this response.
4. Do you feel society is doing enough to prevent predators from harming innocent people, including children?
5. How do you feel about child sex trafficking? Do you want to stop it?
6. What have you done to stop predators in your own life?
7. Do you think stopping predators is just the job of the police, politicians, and religious leaders? Think again.
8. Did you know that the modern slave trade is at its historical worst?
9. Did you see the movie *Sound of Freedom*? Did it move you?
10. What can you do to help the situation?

Seven

GREED

He who is greedy of gain brings ruin on his own
house, but he who hates bribes will live.
— Proverbs 15:27

Greed to me is one of the most common and yet most pivotal sins that
will determine our fate on judgment day. It is written as both a venial sin
as well as a mortal sin. Why both? As with all sins, the degree to which
one takes it makes all the difference. As Reverend Rivera mentioned in
my interview with him, as well as Reverend Heil, "the punishment fits the
crime," and if we "continue to repeat the same sin over and over with no
remorse," it's an unforgivable sin.

The tenth commandment states, "You shall not covet anything that
belongs to your neighbor." This describes desiring to the point of seeking
to take something that is not yours away from someone. This is a core
commandment that leads to all other sins, including theft, murder, lying,
and adultery. *Covet* means to take. It could be a job, a life, money, success,
relationships, friendships; coveting causes havoc in people's lives due to

bearing false witness, evil thoughts, and blasphemies under Jesus Christ's name.

Any thoughts that begin with a negative intention or negative energy will further produce more negative or evil energy. When we give into greed, we will always desire more—we will never be satisfied.

Solomon warned, "He who is greedy for gain troubles his own house" (Proverbs 15:27). And Paul emphasized, "Be content with whatever you have" (Philippians 4:11).

The apostle Paul explained, "But those who desire to be rich fall into temptation and a snare, and into many foolish and harmful lusts which drown men in destruction and perdition. For the love of money is the root of all kinds of evil, for which some have strayed from the faith and their greediness, pierced themselves through with many sorrows" (Timothy 6:9–10). But notice that Paul did not tell us to be lazy and not earn money. The Bible emphasizes that we are not to take what is not ours. Do not be greedy—do not make others suffer because of your greed. That does not mean "don't be successful." It does not mean "don't try to earn money." It means that we are not to take away from or prey on other people.

Many people do not fully grasp this concept of money in the Bible. Everyone is wealthy in the eyes of God. If you have love, you have wealth. If you have food on your table, you are blessed with riches. Be grateful for what you have. If there is something you want, God said He will give it to you. He will make it available to you not by taking it from someone else but by providing opportunities for you to earn it. *Earning* is the key. We ultimately work for God. We have His love, but we must earn the rewards of heaven. There is no favoritism in heaven. God does not favor one person over another. The higher levels of heaven or of glory are reserved for those who have earned them—in essence, they are for those who passed the test.

> But our citizenship is in Heaven, and from it we also await
> a savior, the Lord Jesus Christ. (Philippians 4:17–21)

Heaven is the ultimate home and destination for all of God's creatures. Each one of us has our own journey based upon the lessons we still need to learn—we must understand that to appreciate why people lead different lives. We all have our own unique gifts, as we have our own unique lessons and journeys.

Let me clarify deceptive behaviors in society to further elaborate on this message.

CIA agents identify clusters of deceptive behaviors as far more serious than those of general liars. There is a difference. People lie for many reasons—some for very good reasons. Listen to Pamela Meyer's TED talk on YouTube "How to Spot a Liar." She talks about lies and the degrees of deception. Some lies are intended to not hurt someone's feelings—to say "Oh, nice shirt." But when there are clusters of lies for serious reasons such as fraud, scandals, and theft—this is far different. In some cases, you might notice duper's delight in someone who is antagonistic, such as a sociopath. You may notice that they display narcissistic behaviors that again can range in severity. FBI agents are trained in *lie-spotting* techniques that decode body language. There are even specialized eye trackers and infrared brain scans to detect when someone's lying, although most signs can be caught without equipment if you take note of clusters of these general movements when asking serious questions. Meyer stated, "Yes, we all do generally make gestures that can be dismissed or noted as a sign of anxiety or nervousness for being questioned—but when these signs become clusters and there is an identified number of these signs appearing in short intervals of time it becomes obvious, they are lying." One motion that Meyer identified as particularly alarming during any interview and seen as a red flag is a smile of contempt—a half-smile with lip movement to one side with a cool demeanor. The evil in these traits becomes more heightened and concerning along with the degree of deception. "This is a blatant sign to run for your life!" says Meyer.

Most people feel uncomfortable, for instance, borrowing a dollar to get a soda. Some would take the dollar but would make a point to pay you back immediately. A few wouldn't think twice about it—they'd just take it. And yet another group—an even smaller percentage—would think they are entitled to it. Now let's take this to a larger scale. If people start off in life in one of those groups that would never do it at all, more than likely they have very conscientious minds, were taught ethically and with integrity, and adhere to God's word. Now, if people in the complete opposite group start off that way, how do you think they'll be by the end of their lives? My guess is far, far worse. They never had any morals to begin with. They already felt *entitled*. We know right from wrong as early as age three—that's embedded into the core of *who* we are. It's not always our parents who mold us into the good or bad people we are—we have a choice. This is why some siblings have completely opposite character traits, integrity, and morals.

In my opinion, greed is the most disgusting sin that brings the fire for all other sins. Greed leads to envy, jealousy, stealing, murder, abuse, and all kinds of corruption and lies. The more you get, the more you want and the worse you become as a human being. It is a path to complete darkness. Greedy people not only destroy their own lives, but they also destroy everyone else's in their path. It's like an addiction—they do not know how to stop, and they cannot stop without God's help.

Let's start with greed within a family. One of the biggest issues today as I have witnessed working in health care is elder abuse. Elderly people are vulnerable because of their age and physical deficits. Most cannot hear well, and their vision is poor. Mentally, they are declining. Dementia doesn't just suddenly come on—cognitive impairment is progressive. Average people in their fifties or sixties becomes forgetful occasionally. In their seventies it's even more common to be forgetful. By the time they hit their eighties or nineties, they're in some stage of dementia. There are always exceptions to this rule, but people at this age are not as sharp as they used to be.

Then we have certain children who are needy, codependent, and often lazy or gossipy who never take blame and often wallow in self-pity. We all have someone like that in our families. Over the years I've heard all kinds of character traits and stories leading to the same conclusion—there's one in every family! Watch out for those family members. They are the ones who would feel *entitled* to the dollar for a soda. By the time they hit their sixties, they have masked their deception and have preyed on the mother or father more times than can be counted. The next thing you know, Mom's money is slowly being liquidated. Sometimes those at fault tell lies like, "I needed it to pay my loan for X, Y, or Z." You then find out there was no loan. Then more significant lumps of money go missing—at first a thousand dollars, then five thousand, then twenty thousand, and then over time five hundred thousand dollars disappears, and the inheritance is gone. Then the question is, "How are we going to pay for Mom or Dad's home health aide since they no longer have the money?" If I had a dollar for every time I heard that story, I would be rich myself. But this is an example of real, deceptive, sinful behavior. This crosses the line from venial sin to mortal sin. And this is only an example of what happens in families.

Another scenario could be that one sibling feels that they have done all the work in caring for a parent, so they feel they deserve all the money. This narcissistic behavior is seen all the time. But who is determining who did all the work? Is it that same sibling? People in general see only what they want to see. They see very clearly what they are doing, but do they see what others do? And even so, does doing that work entitle them to coerce the parent into giving them more money or to not refuse it if given more in the end? Are we in a society where we still look out for our family members? Do we even care about our siblings, parents, or children anymore? Do we really know what goes on behind closed doors? Are we really so disingenuous to make a judgment statement that we know what others are doing? Because the truth is that we don't. We only know what we *think* we know. This goes back to St. Augustine's comment in his book *Confessions*: "Many of the things we do may therefore seem wrong to men but are approved in the light of your knowledge, and many men which applaud are condemned in your eyes." Don't be so bold to assume you see with God's eyes. Only He knows the truth.

Now, when we discuss corporations or politics, we are in a whole other ball game. The level of greed that is involved in politics and businesses is completely deceptive for the reasons I mentioned in the previous chapter on *predators*. Keep in mind that politicians have political agendas that come across as sincere and good but that often can and do get abused. For example, collecting donated funds for one cause and transferring them to be used for another cause with different intentions affects the integrity, morals, and characters of those who are involved. The same can be said for corporate leaders who are dismissive of employees who don't agree with their political agenda, religious beliefs, culture, age, sex, or race, and the list can go on. We often see nepotism in the workplace. Women weren't always promoted as quickly as men, even those with the same skill set and education. The Equal Employment Opportunity Commission (EEOC) wasn't established until 1965 in the United States, one year after Title VII of the Act, which prohibits the discrimination of employment on the basis of race, color, religion, sex, or national origin. This isn't too long ago.

Another evil in the workplace is theft: embezzlement, electronic transfer of funds, stock scandals, fraud, money laundering, identity theft, and other types of scams often done on the internet. Again, the degree to which the sin is elevated is the degree to which God will judge. We have Miranda rights in the United States, but there are no Miranda rights with God. It's either *black or white*—meaning good or bad. There is no *gray* or in-between in the end.

Many research studies have been done on greed. In one peer-reviewed research article (Shiyu, Weipeng, Weniwei, et al. 2023), the findings concluded that there was empirical evidence that aggression played a role in the "greed-aggression association"—observed through negative psychopathology, happiness, and gray matter volumes in the prefrontal cortex. These findings improve our understanding of greed and the cognitive and neural mechanisms that may underlie its role in behavioral aggression. This research supports my original statement and the statements of other authors regarding human intentions. Every action begins with a thought. We can't control what others do, but we can control how we react. Education and awareness of our actions are the key to success and understanding. What we do and what we say matter.

Let's hear what our Christian ministry leaders have to say on the issue of greed.

Father Claret:

- "Greed is a capital sin that can be a mortal sin if action is taken."
- "The degree to how greedy a person is or to the extent of their greed determines how far they moved away from Christ."
- "The denial of greed or sin of taking something that doesn't belong to you and not confessing it, or apologizing and not really being remorseful does matter."
- "It then cannot be forgiven."
- "Again, it comes to a complete confession of a condition to repent and the understanding not to do it again."

Reverend Bustillos: "Sin is sin, and there are repercussions regardless."

Reverend Pennella:

- "Greed is a double sin."
- "Greed is the cause of corruption, child sex trafficking, and other horrific acts—money is the motive."

Reverend Krahn: "All sin is straying from God and ultimately keeping you from heaven. Greed or stealing is not different from murder because both keep you out of heaven."

Reverend Hartman: "Greed is the factor that leads to all other sins."

Reverend Boggs: "No matter the sin, you must have remorse to be forgiven."

TAKING INVENTORY

1. Do you believe greed is problematic in society and possibly the root of all sin?
2. Does greed influence your decisions?
3. Does greed play a part in your family?
4. Does greed play a part in your workplace?
5. Do you feel entitled to take what is not yours?
6. Do you have family members whom you cannot trust with money?
7. Have you ever taken what isn't yours or also belongs to your siblings?
8. Have you ever manipulated a parent into giving you money?
9. Do you feel there are consequences for taking money that you haven't earned?
10. What do you feel God's punishment will be for stealing with no remorse?

Eight

ENVY AND JEALOUSY

You shall not worship any other god, for the Lord
is "the Jealous One;" a jealous God is he.
— Exodus 34:14

Envy and jealousy very well lead to destruction. Envy is an emotion of admiration, but if not kept in a healthy perspective, it leads to discontent and jealousy. James 3:16 states, "For where jealousy and selfish ambition exists, there will be disorder and every vile practice."

Let's remember the reason Lucifer became evil in the first place—due to jealousy of God. Lucifer wanted to rule heaven. Well, like Lucifer, humans have the capacity to experience evil within themselves due to thoughts and feelings of jealousy. Sometimes envy motivates us to do better, to have a role model, or to gain a higher achievement. That is healthy, but when the *intention* becomes deceitful, when we want to destroy someone else's job, career, relationship, or financial status due to jealousy—and we see this all around us—it is evil. Just like heaven has many levels, so does hell. The issue is how far some people go to deceive others. Do we really know anyone? People are deceived by their parents, their children, their siblings, their relatives, their friends, their religious leaders, their doctors, their lawyers, their therapists, their coaches, their teachers, their bosses, and their coworkers on a daily basis. Some are very good at detecting deception, while others are blindsided.

There are six types of jealousy: romantic jealousy, rational and reactive jealousy, family jealousy, sexual or suspicious jealousy, power jealousy, and pathological jealousy. The traits of jealous people are fear, resentment, lack of empathy, and lack of self-esteem. The traits of envious people are based on a desire to have something that someone else has, and they can lead to sadness or personal change.

Let me begin by discussing envy. Envy stems from a dissatisfaction with one's self-image. This is why mental health counseling is very important. When people do not know what their gifts are or the reasons they are here in the first place, they can self-destruct. It is important to be raised in a good, loving environment; and if you weren't, then beware that you could transfer any negative emotions, thoughts, and feelings to the next generation. You must focus on why *you* are here. And I will get into that in the upcoming chapters. Throughout my career in health care, particularly mental health counseling, I've come across many clients as well as other therapists who struggle with their purpose, even as they are doing it. That thought, *Am I good enough?* is the pivotal thought the leads to envy and jealousy, particularly with thoughts like, *I want to be like her or him.*

If you don't take pride in who you are as an individual, how can you help anyone else? Love yourself first. If you cannot love yourself, you can't love anyone else. Be kind to yourself because, if you don't, you are vulnerable to these two evils.

Many people, for the most part, recognize their strengths but wish they had this or that. This is normal and somewhat healthy. However, when we attempt to demean, bully, gossip about, exploit, expose, or create a problem with someone out of jealousy or envy, this is where the evil begins. This is not normal. We are truly going into a dark direction once we put those thoughts into action, and remember, everything starts with an intention. In cases like this, which lead to escalated levels of evil, our decisions become so deceitful that we become more and more exposed to negative energy and entities. And I do mean *entities*. God is the one and only protector from the evil one. People who have had NDEs and out-of-body experiences, like *me,* can tell you that the energy of God is unmistakable. But if you do not acknowledge or accept God or Jesus Christ, you are vulnerable to very negative living as well as nonliving energy.

In my opinion, this is why many people struggle through life—and I don't mean just financially. I mean spiritually, emotionally, and physically. These are the ones who somehow just can't get it together. All of heaven always wants to help and guide you through life, but when you choose the dark path, you go astray and are more vulnerable to dark energy. You can call it evil, dark energy, Satan—the bottom line is that it's not good.

Jealousy is especially prominent in families with one sibling who is academically smarter than another—where one went to college and the other didn't—or where one sibling excelled at sports while the another didn't. This happens all the time in families, in almost every family. The degree to which a person acts upon those thoughts of envy or jealousy determines how good or bad a person really is. How far will they go? How destructive will they be in attempting to destroying another's success? Parents can also be blindsided when it comes to certain children, especially children who always seem to need them. They are often seen as the favorites, but in actuality, they are just the neediest —what some experts would call *borderline personalities.* They are the gas lighters of the family, the instigators of trouble, the attention seekers, and often characteristic of having a very low self-esteem. They are the ones from whom everyone will keep a distance and appease just to keep the peace.

The workforce today can also be brutal. People are competitive, and it starts as children. Some never learned how to play nicely in the sandbox. When it comes to the workplace, though, there's a whole different set of rules. Many things have improved, as I mentioned earlier in the book. Women now are closer to equal pay and equal rights and hold high leadership positions, as do all minorities. There is a balance in the workplace, but it seems to have gone to the opposite extreme, where the skill sets don't have to be as equal to make up for the demographic diversities. This also leads to envy and jealousy and a general self-destruction in the sense that fairness just isn't present. Some employees don't work as hard as others, yet the ones who don't work hard are getting promotions. We see that all the time. The point taken here is that, when thoughts arise to create turmoil in the workplace, *what is the intention*? Is it about fairness, or is it for about envy, jealousy, or greed? And how far does it go before it is evil?

Let's see what the research says about envy and jealousy. Of the various studies on the subject, most are designed to determine specific causes or effects of a controlled behavior. According to one research study on friendship jealousy,

> the findings suggest that friendship jealousy is (a) uniquely evoked by third-party threats to friendships (but not the prospective loss of the friendship alone), (b) sensitive to the value of the threatened friendship, (c) strongly calibrated to cues that one is being replaced, even over more intuitive cues (e.g., the amount of time a friend and interloper spend together), and (d) ultimately motivates behavior aimed at countering third-party threats to friendship ("friend guarding"). Even as friendship jealousy may be negative to experience, it may include features designed for beneficial—and arguably prosocial—ends: to help maintain friendships. (Krems, Williams, Aktipis, and Kenrick 2021).

In another study on the resolve of workplace jealousy, the research findings suggest that

> workplace envy has gradually become a hot research topic for organizational behavior. Scholars have explored the antecedents and consequences of envy following the traditional research paradigm. The latest leadership theory also provides new ideas for its development. Although the traditional methods continue to optimize the research on the relationship between leadership and envy, they still do not fully reflect the binary logical relationship between the two and cannot offer sufficient explanatory power for the psychological activities and behaviors of employees and supervisors.... Researchers have come to the conclusion that effective leadership can adjust the existence of various types of envy and transform it into the actual productivity of the workplace. (Liu, Geng, and Yao, 2021).

A study by Yang and Tang found that, as an effect of implementing self-control, "Individuals' striving behavior was only affected by benign envy—while individuals' aggressive behavior was influenced by both malicious envy and self-control. Ego depletion moderated the effect of malicious envy on aggressive behavior."

In a *Psychology Today* article titled "The Psychology and Philosophy of Envy," Dr. Neel Burton wrote,

> To feel envy, three conditions need to be met. First, we must be confronted with a person (or persons) with something—a possession, quality, or achievement—that has eluded us. Second, we must desire that something for ourselves. And third, we must be personally pained by the associated emotion or emotions. I say "personally pained" because it is this personal dimension that separates envy from more detached feelings such as outrage or injustice.... In sum, envy is the personal pain caused by the desire for the advantages of others. In **Old Money**, Nelson W Aldrich Jr describes the pain of envy as, "the almost frantic sense of emptiness inside oneself, as if the pump of one's heart were sucking on air." Envy is mean and miserly, and arguably the most shameful of the deadly sins. Our envy is hardly ever confessed, often, not even to ourselves.... Compared to envy, jealousy is easier to admit to, suggesting that it might be the lesser of the two evils.... Envy is deeply ingrained in the human psyche, and common to all times and people. Our tribal ancestors lived in fear of arousing the envy of the gods, whom they placated with elaborate rituals and offerings. In Greek mythology, it is Hera's envy for Aphrodite that sparked off the Trojan War. In the Bible, it is from envy that Cain murdered Abel, and "through the devil's envy that death entered the world." And in the Hindu *Mahabharata*, it is from "burning envy" that Duryodhana waged war against his cousins the Pandavas.

Let's hear what the Christian ministers have to say about envy and jealousy.

Father Claret:

- "Jealousy and envy are a capital sin, that does lead to a mortal sin once action is taken."
- "The degree to which this occurs does make a difference."
- "There's a difference between feeling jealous and sabotaging someone out of jealousy."
- "Once action is taken it is a mortal sin and it does need to be confessed through the sacrament of reconciliation in order to be forgiven with a condition to repent and an understanding not to do it again."

Reverend Bustillos: "Sin is sin, and there are repercussions regardless of the sin."

Reverend Krahn:

- "The degrees of sin vary amongst themselves, and all sin keeps you from heaven."
- He did note that it is quoted in the Bible regarding the levels of glory, which is heaven.

Reverend Hartman:

- "Jealousy is a 'huge' factor of sin."
- "We have free will to live our lives, but when we have jealousy or envy of someone else—we are not living the life Jesus wanted us to."

Reverend Heil:

- "No deed goes unpunished."
- "With every intention, there is a cause and an effect."
- "There is a balance to the intention or deed."

TAKING INVENTORY

1. How profound is the sin of jealousy in your life?
2. Is jealousy a factor in your workplace?
3. How do you handle jealousy?
4. Do you recognize the difference between envy and jealousy?
5. Do you believe there are ways to avoid jealous reactions?
6. How aware are you of jealousy in others or perhaps yourself?
7. Do you see the sin of jealousy in your own family?
8. If you had to rate the jealousy in your family on a scale of one to ten, what rating would you give it? *That may indicate just how profound a problem it truly is in your life.*

Nine

EMOTIONAL VS. PHYSICAL WRONGDOINGS

The prating of some men is like sword thrusts,
but the tongue of the wise is healing.
— Proverbs 12:18

Emotional and physical abuse is at the forefront of domestic crimes across the globe. It is not limited to family life. It is an evil that dwells within workplaces, religions, cultures, politics, social media, and societies in general. When there is physical abuse, there most certainly is emotional abuse—they go hand in hand in all toxic relationships. Often when abusers cannot abuse their victims in public and get away with it, they will often mentally or emotionally abuse them to demean their character, instill a sense of fear or inferiority in them through intimidation, isolate them, limit their ability or power, diminish their self-confidence, restrict their financial control, attempt to humiliate them, and always deny responsibility and blame the victims, also called gaslighting.

Financial abuse falls under the category of emotional and mental abuse, which were discussed in chapter 7, "Greed." Greed arises from wanting power or control. Diminishing another person's power or control over money is a very common sin in the workplace as well as in families. This is seen not only in romantic relationships but also in parent-child relationships, sibling relationships, friendships, religious relationships, politics, and business relationships. Sometimes it involves showing favoritism to a particular employee, sibling, or child; even as grown adults, parents can hold hostility toward a who was perhaps favored by a deceased blood-related parent or toward a stepchild or adopted child who does not have a good relationship with one parent. Favoritism is an evil that can brew all other sins, especially if it is not recognized or rectified; then the degree of this evil becomes exacerbated. This is probably the most prevalent when it comes to the death of a parent, particularly when family members discover that wills were recently changed to undermine the other heirs. In the workplace, favoritism is often seen in promotions of coworkers who don't deserve them. Sometimes this is due to discrimination based on religious affiliation, sex or gender, race, or disability. Employees get raises or promotions that were not earned, or the opposite may hold true— someone who deserved a raise didn't get it even though the remainder of the department did. Most organizations now have an EEOC office to deter this behavior, but it still exists and does happen every day. In the case of inheritance, specialized attorneys deal with elder abuse and inheritance scandals, where the motivation is always *money.*

As per Wikipedia, "*physical abuse* is any intentional act causing injury, trauma, bodily harm or other physical suffering to another person or animal by way of bodily contact"—this includes sexual abuse, which I will define more in the next paragraph. Physical abuse includes hitting, kicking, pushing, biting, choking, throwing objects, and using weapons—including restraints, confinement, or drugs and alcohol. It can take the form of withholding basic needs such as food, clothing, and medical care, especially if you are the health-care proxy of an elderly person. It also includes the use of psychological trauma by means of instilling fear, creating anxiety, depression, or post-traumatic stress disorder as a result. Physical abuse can occur in any relationship, including those between family members, partners, caregivers, parents, guardians, clergy, teachers, hospital providers, and any and all health-care providers. It can occur in any situation in which one person is deemed officially or unofficially incompetent by others.

Often it happens when adults do not have the capacity to make their own decisions—sometimes it could even be just financial incompetence. Even hearing loss can result in a ruling of incompetence because they cannot fully understand what is happening, while others do not have the memory capacity to recollect conversations days, weeks, months, or years later. People can be manipulated into receiving medical care and making financial decisions they would not ordinarily approve, and the list goes on. Some may be subjective or debatable; *nonetheless,* they are important.

Sexual abuse is another form of physical abuse. It involves the unwanted touch or sexual penetration of another human being. In the cases of minors, it is an affirmative no and serious wrongdoing. It is a criminal activity and is deemed a mortal sin within Christianity across denominations. In the case of adults, it is also deemed a crime if it is not consensual. "No" still means "no," and sexual abuse is a crime. Rape is the most disgusting act next to torture and murder. It is a crime that has become increasingly violent and tolerable in secret societies. It is an evil that is ungodly and unforgivable if not repented with sincere remorse. The sin is despised by society as a whole; yet it still exists and is not spoken about often enough, especially when the sexual crime involves a minor. The movie *Sound of Freedom* is bringing more public discussion of this topic to the table, especially about the underground illegal slave trade that has escalated to the point of surpassing the illegal arms trade. A surplus of whistleblowers have come forward to protest this most horrendous act of violence. Issues such as have existed since before the time of Christ, but there has been no time in recorded history that they have been to this extent and gone to this degree of evil. Advanced technologies, the internet, and funding from elite billionaires who condone and support this wickedness have brought these disgusting acts to new heights—which may very well be the exact turning point for Christ's return. From what I can see, society knows that rapists are getting away with these demonic acts and has resorted to promoting abortions in response rather than going after the perpetrators. It is a cop-out. *Liberal media and politicians claim that we need abortions because of rape.* But we need tougher laws for these kinds of criminals. Killing the innocent is not the answer. In America we are innocent until proven guilty, but with today's technology it is easier than ever to find out who the perpetrators are. We need to focus on stopping them and not being lenient on jail time or releasing them early for good behavior. These kinds of criminals are very hard to rehabilitate—I'd say it's impossible, but anything is possible with God. There is nothing more disheartening than hearing that a person has raped or tortured a child. Judgment is for the Lord, but society does have the power to prevent such crimes. Democratic nations also have trials with a jury of peers to determine the degree of criminal punishment while on earth. God's judgment and our due process of law are two very different understandings—which society needs to get straight.

Mental abuse can be more subtle than emotional abuse, but it does lead to emotional abuse *nonetheless.* Mental abuse is the use of tone and language that is demeaning by nature. Mental abuse, often referred to as *physiological abuse,* focuses on questioning and influencing a person's way of *thinking* and views on reality. Mental abuse can include making unreasonable demands, being overly critical, wanting a partner to sacrifice their needs for others, or causing them to doubt their integrity. It affects how victims think of themselves.

Emotional abuse targets a person's feelings; it uses emotions rather than personal sentiments to manipulate, punish, and achieve control. Emotional abuse is very similar to mental abuse, but it affects how victims *feel* about themselves. This can lead to acts of adultery, which is a mortal sin. Research has demonstrated that, in many cases, people commit adultery because of how their spouses made them *feel.* Believe it or not, it is rarer for adultery to happen out of sheer experimentation or temptation. This does not make the act excusable, however. We need to learn from it and educate others on how to treat one another. Mental health counseling, spiritual counseling, and marriage counseling are key to a sustainable marriage and lifestyle. However, it doesn't end there. People need to understand that there needs to be accountability on all ends, including in the training of therapists. Education is the key—education in the workplace and public schools, education in the churches, and education in the governments and the communities at large. If the general public followed the twelve-step program that is promoted in Alcoholics Anonymous, we'd all do a lot better, especially if the second step were reiterated regularly: "Believe that a Power greater than ourselves could restore us to sanity."

Let's hear what the research has to say about infidelity and broken romantic relationships. There are many studies on this. In one, the research findings indicated for both male and female heterosexual individual relationship barriers were the cause of the infidelity over lust, religion, and demographics (Mark, Janssen, and Milhausen 2011). I've heard this data to be true throughout my entire career in mental health. Without mutual respect in a relationship, regardless of infidelity, the relationship will never be successful. Communication skills are very important—what you say matters, what you do matters, how you make another person feel matters. I'm sure you've heard the saying, "I can't remember what this person did, but I remember how he or she made me feel." This is the truth. At the end of the day, as your life passes by, people will forget the day-to-day memories but hold onto how you made them *feel*.

Both emotional and mental abuse are byproducts of physical abuse. Physical abuse can be absent, but emotional abuse will be present when mental abuse occurs. How we *feel* because of any kind of abuse will be inherently negative. We are human beings made up of emotions—all kinds of emotions. When one has gone through any kind of traumatic event, it is only normal to feel angry, upset, and hurt. Bottling any of our emotions is not healthy, and this is why we will transfer the abuse if we don't get help and release these emotions in a healthy manner. People must seek help when they have been emotionally, physically, or sexually abused. They need a friend, a family member, clergy, a teacher, or any trusted person in their lives to mentor them in their recovery. It is best to seek professional help; however, some are not comfortable with going to just anyone— which is understandable in certain circumstances such as rape—but the victim still must seek some kind of help. Seeking God, prayer, meditation, exercise, a yoga routine, or another holistic remedy is always an alternative to consulting a human. People experience varying degrees of abuse and develop varying degrees of coping mechanisms, which is also important to be aware of. If you aren't aware of your current state, listen to those who are or who have been there. The last thing you ever want to do is to transfer your abuse onto someone else—especially your children.

What has peer-reviewed research determined about the causes of physical and emotional abuse? According to a study titled "Effects of Physical and Emotional Abuse and Its Chronicity on Crime into Adulthood" (Hyunzee, Todd, Jungeun, et al. 2015), physical abuse is both directly and indirectly related to effects of crime, especially on later adult crime.

The article, "Is Emotional Abuse as Harmful as Physical and/or Sexual Abuse?" (Dye 2019) along with previous studies in this research article—concluded that

> emotional abuse may be the most damaging form of maltreatment and cause adverse developmental consequences equivalent to, or more severe than, those of other forms of abuse (Hart et al. 1996)." (Even clergy agree with this, including the Roman Catholic priest.) Those who reported emotional abuse had higher scores for depression, anxiety, stress, and neurotic personality compared to those who reported only physical, only sexual, or combined sexual and physical abuse.

Let's hear what the Christian ministers have to say regarding emotional and physical abuse:

Father Claret:

- "Abuse is a mortal sin and sometimes the emotional abuse can actually be worse than physical abuse."
- "The degree to which sins occur absolutely matters."
- "Physical harm of any human being is a mortal sin."
- "Abortion is viewed by the Catholic church as worse than the killing of an adult human due to the innocence of a child. This is also true of sexual abuse or any abuse of an innocent child. This is viewed by the Catholic church as an evil act."
- "The extent of this mortal sin also varies in degrees and for each occurrence and degree of abuse the sin moves you further and further away from Christ."
- "Again, for forgiveness of a sin—you must have a condition to repent and an understanding not to do it again."

Reverend Bustillos:

- "When there is trauma or abuse of any kind, the sin is always worse—it will draw in the demons."
- "Abortion is equal to murder."

- "There is also sin from ancestors who had commit heinous crimes—sin from bloodlines."
- "When performing exorcisms, a key factor in noting if the person was possessed by a demon or if it is their personality trait to be evil is recognized in the exorcist's execution of prayers. Demons will respond with prayer, but if they don't—it is of their own nature to be evil."

Reverend Krahn:

- "All sin in which there is no remorse will not be forgiven—but through Christ's resurrection if there is remorse and recognition of the sin—it can be forgiven."
- "We are all called to a higher standard as Christians to lead positive lives that elevate the souls of others."

Reverend Pennella: "Harm of any kind is a double sin because it affects another person."

Reverend Hartman:

- "Emotional abuse is often worse than physical abuse."
- "Emotional abuse does affect the way we choose to live our lives, the decisions we make, and so forth."

Reverend Heil: "There is karma in the world, and no one gets away with anything—it will hit them when they least expect it."

Reverend Boggs:

- "Abortion is seen as the same as murder of an adult human being— it is against Eastern Orthodox teachings."
- He says the ancient text "The Didache" states, "You shall not slay the child by abortion," and "You shall not kill what is generated." According to Reverend Boggs, "Other early Christian texts say the same."
- "Orthodoxy has always been against abortion."
- "Child sex trafficking and pedophilia would be considered sins but can be forgiven through repentance."

TAKING INVENTORY

1. Do you recognize mental or emotional abuse?
2. Have you witnessed mental or emotional abuse?
3. Are you aware of the tone and words you use when interacting with others? Do you recognize your intention of action?
4. If someone tells you that they didn't like the way you spoke to them, would you automatically say, "You're too sensitive," or would you be more mindful next time?
5. Do you think that how you respond to someone matters?
6. Are you aware of the signs of physical abuse?
7. Are you aware of the signs of sexual abuse?
8. Do you recognize society's problem with child and human sex trafficking?
9. Were you aware of the modern slave trade?
10. Were you aware that an unborn fetus has nerve endings and *feels* the torture of the abortion?
11. Do you believe people who are found guilty of sexual abuse should be accountable?
12. What do you think helps a pregnant woman *more:* abortion or stricter laws against rapists? Think of the harm of the fetus before answering this question. Many loving and honorable couples who are looking to raise a baby can't conceive one of their own.

Ten

DEATH OF THE BODY—WHAT COMES NEXT?

I know someone in Christ, who fourteen years ago (whether in the body
or out of the body I do not know, God knows), was caught up to the
third heaven. And I know that this person (whether in the body or out of
the body I do not know, God knows), was caught up into Paradise and
heard ineffable things, which no one may utter. About this person I will
boast, but about myself I will not boast, except about my weaknesses.
2 Corinthians 12:2–5

Death is not a subject that most like to talk about, not even the religious;
however, it is part of our reality and culture. In Christ we know we are
saved through Him, and we have eternal life. The soul does not die. I
personally believe it wasn't created when we first were born on the earth
in this lifetime; as Jesus said in scripture, your soul was known to God
before you were in your mother's womb (Jeramiah 1:5): "Before I formed
you in the womb, I knew you; and I ordained you a prophet to the nations."

I am Roman Catholic and of Christian faith; however, I believe we all
have much to learn from one another. Among all religions and religious

beliefs lie truths—truths we can't ignore. Buddha taught that life is beyond our five senses; we are divinely connected to one another as one family, and we feel it in our souls. This makes profound sense. Caroline Myss spoke of the definition of *conscious* in her book *Intimate Conversation with the Divine*. An epiphany is a sudden awakening to another, more vibrant, mystical level of consciousness, leading to a new life path or a divine awakening. Myss states, "We question the existence of God, or deny it entirely because that position allows us to *talk about God* but does not commit us to act with conscience engaged." If we are to say we believe in God, in heaven, and in all the wonders that God has created, we must accept the fact that there are supernatural experiences all over the world, and they are not limited to only one religion, one culture, one race, or one living being. Every living being is entitled to God's grace. And only with grace do our beliefs penetrate our souls. So we must understand that, when divine light flows through us, that is our energy, our life-force energy given only to us from God. In that state of peace and understanding we must recognize that we are all connected to God, who is every living thing's life-force energy. Energy healing comes from God—that is grace. Energy healing only comes from the divine—no one else. All that is good comes from God.

There are many stories of the mystics, in addition to the story of Fatima and that of Conchita at Garabandal discussed earlier. Yet another mystifying apparition of the Blessed Mother appeared to St. Marie-Bernarde Soubirous, also known as Bernadette—she saw the first of her eighteen visions in the Lourdes Church in France on February 11, 1858. On February 25, 1858, "the Lady" told Bernadette to drink the water of the spring that flowed under a nearby rock. Bernadette didn't see a spring but began to dig into the ground, and a day or two later, water began to flow. Bernadette drank this water and bathed in it, as did others, and it acquired a reputation for healing. Not all are healed by this water—only those with deep faith and those who believe it can heal them. Many have been cured of terminal illnesses due to their faith. According to the story, the Lady told Bernadette to have the priests build a church next to this grotto, and since then it has drawn in many crowds from all over the world. The water flows at a rate of thirty-two thousand gallons per day, and the water is shipped all over the world, especially to shrines like the Eastport

Shrine—Our Lady of the Island on Long Island. Bernadette said there's no specific amount of water that must be used, as "just one drop suffices." Through the years, the church has been subjected to much scrutiny, but despite it all, Bernadette was beatified in 1925 and canonized in 1933. Pilgrims from all over the world continue to flock to Lourdes, France, in hopes of being healed. You can read more about this story on the History Today website (http://www.historytoday.com).

At the Eastport Shrine, there is still talk of miraculous healings after using the water that is sold there from the Lourdes Grotto. While I was working as a therapist at the Veteran's Administration Medical Center, I had a patient who had been told she would not walk again. I treated her with individual recreational therapy services, often implementing guided meditation, and one day when I asked her if she'd like to try Reiki. While I prayed and implemented a *laying on of hands*, I noticed a bottle of the Lourdes Grotto healing water. The patient said her aunt had brought it in for her. After the Reiki session, she claimed she felt so light again, like something had lifted from her. She became more enthusiastic regarding physical therapy and her other therapy appointments, and before I knew it, she was being discharged. She walked out of the hospital. It truly was a miracle to witness.

Many stories of the mystics and NDEs are truly miracles of God. They cannot be explained or debunked by society or religious leaders. Those who experience these supernatural events know that they happened. They are not flukes or fairy tales. They serve no other purpose than to provide comfort and serenity to those here on earth, to reassure us that there is a God and that heaven is real, and to remind us to lead a good life—because it does matter.

One of my favorite authors is Ned Dougherty, author of *Fast Lane to Heaven*. In his midthirties he had an NDE. He died on the way to the hospital after having a heart attack; in fact, he went in and out of consciousness in the hospital several times, having recurring NDEs. In his encounter with the heavenly angels, the Blessed Mother, and Jesus, Ned found himself in complete joy and peace while in heaven, but he was falling into darkness prior to calling out for Jesus's help. Without Jesus, we cannot be saved. We have the free will to accept Him or not. Once Ned called out to Jesus, his soul went into the light, and he was shown magnificent things in heaven. He saw a tunnel with crystal-like liquid sparks that danced in a profusion of brilliant colors, synchronized with sounds of crystal-like chimes. This is not uncommon for NDEs—many describe seeing and sensing the same kind of things. Ned spoke of a tunnel of massive energy that assisted and directed his travel. His travel to heaven started with a brilliant golden light that he believed was his creator, God. The light had so much love for him, more than he had ever known on earth. The love and the light were beyond description; no human words could describe. This, again, is not uncommon. He stated that God's love bestowed upon him a cleansing and purification of his spirit. He felt reborn. He further explained in his book that he felt God imbued him with the knowledge of the universe. He felt this knowledge was absorbed and then penetrated the core of his being. Within the knowledge God bestowed upon him were universal laws and revelations that were part of God's plan for the universe. He stated that our memory as physical beings is limited, and when we return to earth, we do not have the capacity to retain such knowledge. Prior to Ned's NDE he was not living a good life. He owned a nightclub, used drugs, and hung out with people who were not good. His NDE changed all that, and he turned his life around, which is very similar to other people's NDEs.

Subsequently, after Ned's NDE, he was shown visions from the Lady of the Light—the Blessed Mother. These visions and apparitions came continuously for some time. Ned was shown that all things have energy in them—the plants, the trees, the roots, and branches of trees—all have God's light in them. Everything is interconnected by a greater design and source of energy. Everything communicates with everything else. All of nature is in harmony with God's plan. God's influence on the earth could be seen and manifested by observing anything in nature. In the future, after the Second Coming, there will be a new world, and Ned was shown that it will be wonderful. There will no longer be death as there is here on earth; we will simply have a transitioning process in our soul's journey.

Personally, I have always seen our life here on earth since the time I was a child as a lesson in school. It's not the main piece of our souls' journey—just an important lesson to sustain us through eternity. Many religions like to clearly state how many lifetimes we have on the earth—I don't think it's important. The important thing is that we learn. If we don't learn our lessons, we cannot move on to the next level. God didn't give us all the answers to all our questions for a good reason, I'm sure. Trust God and focus on today.

What moved me about Ned's book the most was his discussion of the "rock" at the Eastport Shrine on Long Island. This is where I live and go to pray quite often—for more than thirty years I have visited this exact site Ned mentioned in his book. The Eastport Shrine was established by the Montfort Missionaries, a group of priests and brothers founded in France, inspired by the works of St. Louis Marie de Montfort. Montfort was recognized by the Roman Catholic Church for his prophetic visions of the end of times. The property for the Eastport Shrine was donated by the Vigliotta family, farmers, and landowners in Eastport. Bill Vigliotta was in the Montfort Missionaries in the 1950s when the land was donated.

Ned claimed the Blessed Mother had described a place up high on a hill overlooking a body of water on Long Island, and he came across this sacred place while driving in the vicinity of his home in the Hamptons. Ned did not see it as coincidence—more as a calling. In the clearing he recognized the Eastport Shrine as the site of one of his visions of the future with the Blessed Mother. He even had apparitions of the Blessed Mother while there. Now Ned is in his eighties, and he still conveys messages from the Lady of the Light that you can read online on the End of Times Daily.

All of these people who have had NDEs claim to have had life reviews. Life reviews allow each soul to relive in detail with much more knowledge and perspective the life they led, see how they interacted with other people, understand how their interactions were received and felt by others, and learn how they could have done better. They are also shown how much love and goodness they brought to the world and how the good they have done spreads endlessly like a pebble that is thrown into a pond and creates a ripple. Everything we do in this life matters. My whole point in writing this book is to help people recognize that before it is too late.

Another NDE story is from Dr. Mary C. Neal. She had an NDE while on a trip to South America when she was in a kayaking accident. It was estimated that her body was underwater for about a half hour, so she received no air—resulting in a long-term recovery that should have ended her life. It was a miracle she lived through it. She describes in detail how she felt her consciousness in two places at once. She was pinned under her kayak and fighting for her life and then lying under the water lifeless, while at the same time she was enjoying the serenity and encounters of spiritual beings in heaven. Her story is on YouTube, and she wrote two books, *To Heaven and Back* and *7 Lessons from Heaven*. Dr. Neal claims she was greeted by spiritual beings that took her to heaven, where she met Jesus. She was a Christian by faith but was not as dedicated to Christ as she felt she should have been. Being a doctor, she had a busy schedule, but her experience led her to a much stronger belief in God, so she is no longer afraid of death. Her experience also resulted in her having knowledge of future events, including the death of her son—which took place years after her own NDE. She felt that having her experience made her a better doctor—more compassionate and understanding of patients' needs and able to reassure her patients that there really is no death. She continues to speak publicly about her experience on TEDx programs, TV conferences, and discussions. Her visions from heaven are like Ned's in that she felt complete peace and serenity. She did not want to leave heaven and in fact was upset she had to return, even though she knew she had young children at home. All of heaven reassured her that if she were to stay, her children would be OK. Dr. Neal states, "No matter what we do or didn't do on this earth, we are in God's grace....We are fully embraced by grace; you are cradled in the place where healing begins."

Marv Besteman shared the story of his NDE in the book *My Journey to Heaven*. Besteman described his experience in heaven in complete detail, making readers feel like they lived it. It was one of the most captivating books I've ever read about heaven—and definitely one of my favorites. Besteman described his encounter with the apostle Peter at the gates of heaven. He spoke about what it was like waiting in the line to enter the gates and how happy and peaceful everyone was. He described the music, lights, and colors of heaven in explicit detail and stated that he marveled over all that he saw, heard, and felt. He made a point to state that people of all ages were waiting to enter heaven, not just old people. Many young people and babies were waiting in line, reflecting that life on earth is not about growing old; it's about experiencing earth for a specific purpose, and when that purpose is over, we return home to God. Heaven is our true home.

Another author, John Burke, talks about hundreds of NDEs in his book

Imagine Heaven. He makes a point to comfort readers by reassuring us that pets go to heaven too; they were seen playfully running in God's gardens. He was also shown where the children play and how Jesus ministers to them, and all around the children were beautiful animals. Everything in heaven was glorious and full of love. Even lions were present, but they were completely safe to the children and all of heaven. No person or animal there was dangerous. It was a completely harmonious place where past relationships thrived, all to fulfill God's purpose free from the earth's curse of decay and destruction. Burke dedicates many paragraphs and chapters to demonstrating that those who serve the least of God's children will be rewarded. People who have been marginalized, mocked, and outcast are God's children too, and to serve them is very important. No deed goes unnoticed. We have a life review, and in it we are shown our strengths and weaknesses. We are shown how we could have done better and what we did very well. We are reminded that money did not matter; what mattered was how honest we were with it, how hard we worked to earn it, and what we did with it—how we cared for our families and children and how generous we were. Burke also emphasized the importance of working and having a good attitude toward our jobs. We need to look at everything as if we were working for God. Laziness, dishonesty, and slack—God sees all that too!

Betty J. Eadie wrote *Embraced by the Light* about her own NDE. In 1973, Betty died following surgery and returned to tell her story. She told of a vivid recollection of her NDE, claiming to have seen her body in more than three dimensions after leaving it. She was able to see herself from every angle possible all at once—noticing features she's never seen before. She claims three men appeared at her bedside wearing robes of virtue, and a flow emanated from them. As in Dr. Neal's story, these spiritual beings or guides met her, and their communication was rapid and complete but not done verbally—telepathy is the only word to describe it, she says. Other people who have had NDEs say the same. She describes the movement of leaving the earthly plane as being of tremendous speed. I can attest to this from my own out-of-body experience, in which I left my body in a semisleep. I wouldn't say I had a near-death experience, but then again it could have been. The speed at which the soul travels is faster than light or sound or any means that scientists can identify. Eadie goes on to say in her book that she went through a tunnel as well. She experienced a blackness like no other, but it did not cause her fear. In this dark tunnel, she sensed that other souls were going through it as well, but she did not have a connection to them. She sensed all were in complete peace. At the end of the tunnel was a radiant light, white and extensive. She felt the most unconditional love she had ever felt, and she felt as though she were finally home. This is not uncommon to hear either. This is why I am certain that our souls are not created at the time of our birth or conception. This concept of knowing that we are "home" tells me we were in heaven before we were born on earth—undoubtedly.

Here's the story of my out-of-body experience, previously published in my first book, *Mind, Body, Spirit and Discovering the Purpose of Life*.

> "One of the things I never truly understood was how God and spirits can be in two places at once. I had read about this in many books, and it was not until recently that I was shown how this can be from the lord. My out of body experiences have always occurred at night. I usually do fall into a deep sleep and had many dreams of loved ones that I had lost and crossed over on the other side. This experience was quite different. I was sleeping and although my eyes were closed, I could see my husband lying next to me as I was sleeping on my side facing him. My husband was in a deep sleep, and in my thoughts... I was asking God 'How can we be in two or more places at once?' I was not given the answer in words... but he showed me... My spirit lifted out of my body which was frozen stiff and asleep; just very subtly hovering over my body—not exactly fully out yet. I could see my husband lying next to me, quicker than an instant my spiritual body was hovering over the front lawn in the same position.... Not moving... and I was fully aware my spiritual body was the same size and shape as my physical body.... I could see the blades of grass in such perfect detail as I hovered there. Then I was back hovering over my physical body again, looking at my husband—it went back and forth like this a couple of times. Just taking in

the moment as if time had stopped. I was a little confused as to what was happening, but I understood that it was God showing me this. I was very aware I was not dying... I knew it was a lesson. I knew God was showing me something. Then I was able to see myself hovering over the grass and hovering over my physical body in my bed beside my husband at the same time. It was an awe dropping experience, but it made sense. In the spiritual world I understood the law of physics does not apply here. Science will never be able to define this because it is not a physical world. To define the spiritual world using only what you know to be true of the physical world will not work. But I will tell it did happen, and I will tell you the spiritual world does exist."

I also included a second out-of-body experience in that book.

"This time lying flat on my back, in a semi-sleep. I was fully conscious that I was sleeping at the time. I sometimes have trouble sleeping and getting into a comfortable position due to suffering from cervical stenosis and herniated discs in the neck. I live with some element of pain every day of my life... but at night it is much worse finding a comfortable position that won't trigger a massive neck and head pain. I usually sleep with a heating pad to reduce pain and to release the tension in the muscles of my neck. Well, this night, I'm lying on my back and as I am getting very comfortable and relaxed, I go into a deeper sleep I am fully aware it is not a dream as I feel my spirit quickly leave my body. I had God in my thoughts... and I am communicating with God through mental telepathy. As I leave my body my spirit raises up very quickly... I go through the ceiling and roof of my house as my bedroom is on the second floor of the house, but it is too quick for detail. The speed at which the spirit can move is more than can be explained in a physical existence. I am way up high into the solar system, going through the universe I am passing many galaxies of stars and solar systems. From the moment my spirit left my body God was with me the entire time, his presence was surrounding me and protecting me from any kind of harm. I felt fully and completely safe, with no worry or concern. I did not believe I was dying—I had this understanding as I did in my previous out of body experience that God wanted to show me something. As I accelerated into the universe God showed me that there are windows where we can get a glimpse of heaven, while not exactly entering heaven. I was in space the entire time. I understood and God showed me the light in the distance as the gateway to heaven, but God said I could not go there—if I entered there that would be the point of no return. I wasn't afraid to go there, but completely understood my life on earth was not over. I understood God had a purpose for my life, that life and everyone's life on earth is so important. That was like a law. Not that God wouldn't forgive anyone that committed suicide, I don't want anyone to ever think that. God is all loving and all forgiving, so have no worries... I know that is not true. However, if someone does commit suicide what I am very aware of is that your purpose and lessons would not be complete and that means more learning. Getting back to the windows of heaven...God showed me that the soul's life in heaven is similar-to that of heaven in that we spend time with our loved ones, we sit around and talk, not using our mouth. Through mental telepathy we comprehend every word, regardless of what language we use here on the earth. The things we enjoyed here, we will enjoy there, minus all the stressors—*thank goodness*! I remember observing people that were not familiar to me, and people that seemed vaguely familiar to me. My father had passed away in 2001, and the last window I saw was getting a view of the back of his body. He did look of solid substance, not like a ghostly figure that is portrayed in movies or on TV. I would say he looked around the age of thirty-three. He was very young and was sitting in a living room with my ancestors. I did not know or meet any of these ancestors on the earth plane, but it was like having instant knowledge that these souls that my father was with, were my ancestors. My father did not initially know I was there, he was a bit surprised—I knew he felt my presence watching him. He stood up, turned around and said, 'What are you doing here?... It isn't your time!' He didn't mouth these words—the communication was through mental telepathy. He then saw God's presence behind me—what I believe... and seemed to understand it was *just a visit*. In that instant I went back into my body. That was not the first time I had a visitation with my father. But when I do, he always looked around that age of 33."

According to Wikipedia, an estimated *nine million* people in the United States have reported having an NDE, according to a 2011 study in *Annals of the New York Academy of Sciences*. In a 2019 study, "Near-Death Experiences in Medicine," researcher Jonathan Kopel found that NDEs occur in 10 percent to 20 percent of patients who have come close to death and consist of vivid, subjective experiences that occur during life-threatening emergencies. Kopel states in his abstract that "patients who have experienced an NDE show significant transformation in their spiritual and emotional lives, with many stating a renewed sense of meaning, existential awareness, and mystical experiences. Family and friends of patients who have experienced an NDE also report increased comfort, hope, and inspiration. Overall, NDEs have positively impacted the medical profession and physician-patient interactions and represent a growing paradigm shift beyond the naturalistic interpretations of science and medicine." More and more people are coming forward with their stories as science is now open to studying patients' experiences after resuscitation. People are less afraid than in the past to be debunked or labeled with some type of mental disorder as a result of admitting to this experience. Thousands of research studies today are trying to find concrete evidence on the existence of consciousness outside the body. However, much of science still doesn't want to incorporate God in the equation.

Dr. Clifford Lazarus wrote an article in *Psychology Today* in 2019, "Can Consciousness Exist Outside the Body?" He cited the research of Dr. Peter Fenwick, a highly regarded neuropsychiatrist who has been studying the human brain, consciousness, and the phenomenon of NDEs for fifty years. Fenwick believes that consciousness exists independently and outside of the brain as an inherent property of the universe—but he does not give God any credit. In Fenwick's view, according to Lazarus, the brain does not create or produce consciousness; rather, it filters it. For example, he stated that the eye filters and interprets only a very small sliver of the electromagnetic spectrum, and the ear registers only a narrow range of sonic frequencies. He further explains that the eye can see only the wavelengths of electromagnetic energy that correspond to visible light. But the entire electromagnetic spectrum is vast and extends from extremely low energy, long-wavelength radio waves to incredibly energetic, ultrashort-wavelength gamma rays. He says that, while we can't see much of the electromagnetic spectrum, we know things like X-rays, infrared radiation, and microwaves exist because we have instruments for detecting them. He further adds that, when the eye dies, the electromagnetic spectrum does not vanish; it's just that the eye is no longer viable and therefore can no longer react to light energy. But the energy it previously interacted with remains. He further adds that, when the ear dies or stops transducing sound waves, the energies that the living ear normally responds to still exist. He claims that, just because the organ that filters, perceives, and interprets a phenomenon dies, the phenomenon itself does not cease to exist. It only ceases to be in the now—"dead brain" but continues to exist independently of the brain as an external property of the universe itself. He sums it up by stating, "Our consciousness tricks us into perceiving a false duality of self and other when in fact there is only unity. We are not separate from other aspects of the universe but an integral and inextricable part of them. And when we die, we transcend the human experience of consciousness, and its illusion of duality, and merge with the universe's entire and unified property of consciousness." In his conclusion, he says that "only in death can we be fully conscious."

Let's hear what the Christian ministers have to say about the afterlife and people's stories of NDEs.

Father Claret:

- "Scripture states our bodies are made with spirit and soul at once. We cannot have one without the other."
- "In death the earthly body is transformed into a new one—it does not die but is transformed. It is the same body."
- "You then go to a place of purification before you enter heaven."
- In discussion of light phenomena, Father Claret stated, "This can and does happen in prayer particularly while praying the Rosary that we do see light—this phenomenon happens when we are moving with the light of Christ."
- "Our main focus is how we live our lives—living with Christ within us, our relationship with God."
- As far as NDEs and out-of-body experiences, he stated, "I have heard of these experiences." He does not deny the phenomena.
- "We do get second chances in various ways that are life changing."

Reverend Bustillos: He says that, yes, he has heard of others having near-death experiences or out-of-body experiences.

Reverend Pennella:

- "Yes, I have heard of near-death experiences."
- "There was a parishioner who had a heart attack, and after speaking with him regarding his experience—it was a very believable story."
- He believes that God always gives us second chances.

Reverend Boggs:

- "I have worked with people at the end stage of life in hospice and many hospitals."
- "I believe near-death experiences are real."
- He had an out-of-body experience himself as a boy of twelve years of age.

- "Near-death experiencers find themselves in the presence of God where there is nothing but peace and love, and they do not want to leave."
- Reverend Boggs believes that "heaven is waiting for all of us one day" and that "hell is merely a control tactic used by the church to keep people in line."
- "Our modern understanding of hell has been deeply twisted from what Jesus actually spoke about and has nothing to do with His understanding of the topic." Regarding Fatima and the apparitions of the Blessed Mother at Garabandal, Reverend Boggs said he cannot comment on the certainty of those apparitions, as they were not relevant to Eastern Orthodox Christians, but he would not rule them out either. He did state, however, that "Eastern Orthodox Christians have had many experiences and visions of the Holy Theotokos Mary."

Reverend Krahn:

- "Once you pass away, you're in the glorified state of heaven."
- "Heaven is a gloried state."
- When questioned on his thoughts of our Holy Mother being our only mother in heaven and how that changes the relationship with our earthly families, he said that the reality of it is that he'd like to think that his original family, his mother, would still be recognized as his mother."
- Regarding the apparitions by Conchita of Gonzalez, Spain, and Fatima (which he has visited), he says, "The phenomena is not to be ignored—extraordinary things do happen."

Reverend Hartman:

- When asked for his comments on NDEs, he stated, "My grandfather had a near-death experience—I believe it was authentic." "Consciousness is the soul."
- "However, near-death experiences are not discussed in ministry."

Reverend Heil: Reverend Heil is also a psychic medium and has had paranormal experiences. She has had two NDEs as well as out-of-body experiences. She states, "I assure you they are real." She has a YouTube channel where you can learn more about her ministry work. Reverend Heil does interfaith ministry work by counseling others on bereavement and loss as well. She channels through Archangel Michael and has the gift of healing others through her spiritual counseling sessions, ministry, and mediumship. She has the gifts of clairvoyance, clairsentience, clairaudience, and claircognizance. Heil assures others that there is an afterlife and urges them to keep faith in Christ. She also warns, "Hell is real too—and we are given that choice as well. We are responsible for our actions here on the earth." Reverend Heil has visited Fatima and claims, "The energy is fabulous!" She says it is "breathtaking," adding, "There is much faith there." She loved meeting the blue nuns and said, "The water is miraculously healing there."

TAKING INVENTORY

1. Do you understand what a near-death experience is?
2. Do you feel that NDEs are merely dreams, fantasies, or imaginings of the dying brain? If so, how do you explain how people's consciousnesses knew what was happening in the world so accurately when they were clinically dead?
3. Have you ever had an unexplained phenomenon?
4. What do you believe happens to you immediately after the death of your physical body?
5. Do you truly believe and trust you will meet Jesus Christ after your death?
6. If you're a Christian and mock people who talk about their heavenly visits during their NDEs, do you really think you're a true follower of Christ? Think about that.

Eleven

THE FIRST EARTH AGE, LOST BOOKS OF THE BIBLE, ARCHANGELS, FALLEN ANGELS, AND ALIENS

God made the dome, and it separated the water above the dome
from the water below it. God called the dome the sky.
— Genesis 1:7–8

The book of Enoch is very controversial among scholars. It is not accepted in many religious churches due to the inability to verify the information it contains, although much of the text seems aligned to the books of Daniel and Revelation. Enoch is referenced in other writings, including the book of Jubilee, which was canonized in the Ethiopic Christian Church, and the book of the Giants, in which one of the fallen angels is called by the name of Gilgamesh. Enoch was a prophet of God who had written of future events in the world to come after AD 70. He was declared a fake; was rejected by Hilary, Jerome, and Augustine; and was subsequently lost to Western Christianity for over a thousand years (Lumpkin, 2011). However, not all had abandoned the book—the apocryphal book of the Epistle of Barnabas makes many references to and quotes from the book of Enoch. Tertullian (AD 160–230) called the book of Enoch "holy Scripture." The Ethiopian Christian Church holds the book of Enoch as part of its spiritual canon—it was also widely known and read in the first three centuries following Christ's death and resurrection. These ancient manuscripts were found in the caves of Qumran. The Dead Sea Scrolls were penned in the second century BC and were in use until the destruction of the second temple in AD 70. Fragments of the Old Testament were also found in these caves (Lumpkin, 2011).

The first book of Enoch was a composite of several manuscripts authored by many, over a period of three to four hundred years. It was divided into various books—the Book of the Watchers; the Book of the Parables; the Book of Astronomy and Calendar; the Book of Visions; and the Books of Warnings and Blessings of Enoch. Later editions included the Book of Noah. The First Book of Enoch—the Book of the Watchers—is probably the most fascinating in relation to what could be aliens in the skies. The Watchers—also known as the Nephilim, the Eljo, Giants, and big humans—are a group of angels sent to earth to record and teach, but they disobeyed God and fell by their own lust and pride into a demonic state. According to Lumpkin's book, research discovered that it was said that God cleaned the earth of sins of the flesh, but the spirits of the evil Watchers and their accursed offspring *cannot* die. Is this to indicate they may be earthly demons or perhaps our modern-day aliens that roam our skies in UFOs? No one knows for sure, but the book informs God's descendants to watch out for what takes place in the skies, look out for the seasons, observe, and see how His creation changes through the calendar year. Lumpkin suggests that certain passages—Deuteronomy 11:26–28, Genesis 6:1–3, Jude 1:5–6, Genesis 5:32–6:6, Jubilee 7:21–25, Jasher 2:19–22—coincide with the literature taken from this First Book of Enoch. Chapter 7 speaks of how the angels fell and how the Watchers began to impregnate women on the earth, and it also tells the story of the Giants, who had turned against humans and devoured them. The Lord then decided to destroy them because of all the sinfulness on the earth; this is reflected in Genesis 6:7, 8:22, and 9:1. Lumpkin's book goes into great detail on the Watchers and the Giants. Some of these fallen angels have become known as *disembodied spirits*—as the text describes—and do roam the earth; however, the most powerful of the fallen angels are bound in Hades. The book of Enoch also includes the War Scroll, which interestingly enough contains rules for the military, religious preparations, and how the fighting must be conducted. *The Great Rejected Texts* includes lost scripture of the Old Testament, apocalyptic writings, and discussion of the end of days. It also includes lost scriptures of the New Testament, such as the Gospel of Philip, Gospel of Mary Magdalene, apocryphon of John, Gospel of Thomas, Gospel of Judas, and Acts 29.

So who are these fallen angels? They are angels who rebelled against God and were cast out of heaven. They are demons and are responsible for the evil in the world. This is a list of many fallen angels, but it is not a complete list.

> Abaddon is the angel of death and destruction.
> Adramelec is a former archangel.
> Amezyarak, often called Semyaza, is the leader of the Watchers.
> Allocen is the duke of hell.
> Abezethibou is a fallen one-winged Red Sea angel.
> Allocen is a duke in hell.
> Amduscias appears as a unicorn.
> Amon is a strong marquis over forty legions.
> Amy is a president in hell.
> Andras is a marquis who appears raven-headed.
> Andrealphus can transform humans into birds.
> Andromalius appears as a man holding a serpent.
> Apollyon is a fallen angel of death, same as Abaddon.
> Armaros teaches the "resolving of enchantments."
> Asmodayis a king with three heads: a bull, a ram, and a man.
> Asmodeus is one of the evilest fallen angels and an archdemon.
> Astaroth is a grand duke in hell.
> Azael cohabited with women.
> Azazel has a name that means "God strengthens."
> (Lumpkin, 2011).

Lumpkin's book also provides a list of the archangels and heavenly angels who were obedient to our Lord, Jesus Christ. Make no mistake—you are protected by the Lord Jesus Christ as long as you choose Him, so have faith in Christ. As you pray to God and Jesus Christ, ask for the assistance of the archangels. They are very powerful and will protect you. Here is a list, although it may not be complete. You can research more information in Lumpkin's *The Book of Enoch*.

These are the seven most powerful archangels of God's creation:

Archangel Michael is a warrior whose role is to bring protection to us. He provides courage, strength, and justice.

Archangel Raphael is responsible for healing physical and mental ailments.

Archangel Gabriel is known as the angel of communication. He plays the role of God's messenger.

Archangel Jophiel is responsible for guiding you to see the beauty in all things by redirecting your perception back to love.

Archangel Ariel is responsible for protecting the earth and its resources and inhabitants.

Archangel Azrael helps the diseased transition into the spirit realm.

Archangel Chamuel is responsible for bringing peace to the world. He is capable of restoring order and chaotic situations. (Lumpkin, 2011)

There are more archangels and other heavenly angels with very specific jobs and roles in heaven—too many to list in this text. Again, you can find more information in Joseph Lumpkin's book *The Book of Enoch*.

Let's get a better understanding of the three earth ages to understand the earth's age and that each age leads into another. I always liked reading Shepard's Chapel—they do a pretty good job of explaining this in simple terms. On the Bible Study for Life website, an article titled "The Three Earth Ages" by Pastor Murray explains in detail:

> The scriptures tell us of three worlds ages: the world that was, being the spiritual pre-flesh world; the world that is now, or as we know it to today: and the world to come, or the third world of eternity.
>
> **The World That Was**: The world age that was (the first world age) means in (the spiritual world we were with God). We have been given two facts concerning the world that was. In Ezekiel 28, Satan rebelled against God, drawing one third of God's children to follow him and they stood against God in a battle. Satan's pride was his downfall, he stopped loving God and he wanted to be God himself.
>
> Roman 11, In the first earth age, there was a remnant that stood with God against Satan in the first earth age. In the last days there will be 7,000 (from all races) out of that remnant that the Father chose as His very elect to stand against Satan again in the last days. Satan will be cast out of heaven and will deceive the whole world, if possible, the very elect.
>
> Then, of course, the rest of God's children that remained, what of them? The elect stood loyally with God, but some took the path of least resistance, doing nothing, not wanting to get involved in controversy.
>
> Satan shall not be forgiven, but his rebellion posed two choices that God might use for correction. God needs to know if they would love Him or Satan. God could have destroyed all those who stood with Satan or He could

regain their love and forgive them and give His children free will, this is why we are in this earth age.

God would not accept the first choice as He is a loving and merciful God, and these were His children, created by Him. Being an all-powerful God, He could not force their love, but He needs to know if you love Him. Love must come from the heart, given as a free will gift, to have value. Forced love is worthless. The world that is now, as we know it, is His plan for salvation.

The father chose His very elect before the foundations of this world. It is our thought that the elect are those who took a firm stand against Satan in the world that was and perhaps even volunteered for services in this world. The elect are referred to as the first fruits.

Genesis 1:1 In the beginning God created the heaven and the earth.

Notice a period follows this sentence, indicating a statement. This was an accomplished fact. God created the world. This is the world that was, in which the people or souls were in the spirit bodies as opposed to the flesh bodies. It was this world that Satan's rebellion took place.

Genesis 1:2 And the earth was without form and void: and darkness was upon the deep.

The word was in the Hebrew is "tohu va bohu," which means and should have been so translated "became". The only possible deduction from this is that God destroyed the world that was.

The Three Earth Ages by Pastor Murray, The Shepherd's Chapel Booklet Yahveh's Scriptural Plan.

The World That Is Now: Second world age is now. Genesis 1:2 And the spirit of God moved upon the face of the water. This then concerns a new or renewed world.

Refer to Genesis 1:26–28 These verses tell us God created man and woman, as we know them in the flesh body, whom He told to multiply and replenish the earth "a reference to the renewed world or this world that is now. Refer to 2 Peter 3:5–13 which speaks of the "world that perished".

Therefore, God created this world that is now, placing all the souls into flesh bodies, with the exception of Satan. They were and are totally in ignorance of Satan's battle and their own loyalties at that time, so that they might have the opportunity to develop their loyalties anew; in other words, to exercise their free will. Without the hindrance of pre-knowledge, their choice to worship God or their choice to worship Satan would be completely unhampered, given in love and free will.

Satan, the splendid, shining soul, remained in the spirit form with limited yet obvious supernatural powers and was allowed to roam the earth. The reason for this was that Satan was to be used as a tool of deception. Satan's main purpose in this world is to tempt us all away from God, our Living Father and Creator. The Father purposed this, as He wants us to love and worship Him of our own free will. Satan is the catalyst. It is our choice whether we follow God or follow Satan. And this is the reason for this world that is now, as we know it today.

The Three Earth Ages by Pastor Murray, The Shepherd's Chapel Booklet Yahveh's Scriptural Plan.

The World to Come: Revelation chapters 20, 21 and 22, the third earth age to come. Let it suffice to say that the thousand-year period of teaching, the millennium, will be established by Christ upon His return on that "great and dreadful day," which is last day of this age. This marks a new beginning toward spiritual perfection when all shall bow the knee to Christ, as all shall be taught the full truth, when Satan shall be bound in the pit and without influence until he is loosed for the final short season when each one, having been taught the full truth, chooses of his own free will.

The third world age represents eternal life, or the world that is to come. The millennial age will be ended at this time. Revelation 20:13–15 for those who choose to worship Satan: Decisions will have been made that lead to total destruction in the lake of fire. Revelation 21:27 for those who choose to worship the Father, God, through His son, Christ. The millennial age has ended and Revelation 21:1 speaks of a new meaning renewed, refurbished, in other words, a cleansed and holy heaven and earth. This is the eternal Kingdom.

Now, much shall happen in the last days of this age, as we approach the millennium, and these things are of supreme important to the very elect. They would like to read more on the signs of the end. Matthew 24, Mark 13, and Luke 21 will bring us to the Lord—day which is the millennium.

Now, how does this all relate to UFO sightings, ministers' interpretations, and human experiences with aliens here on the earth? Well, the government is now making a slow release of information on these topics more than ever before in history. As you will hear, some ministers express their opinions, and others will tell you exactly what the church's stance is on this. We do know that the Vatican has one of the world's largest telescopes; and different Roman Catholic priests may give you various explanations but nothing that is proven. If you have not listed to Tucker Carlson's interview with scientist Dr. Gary Nolan, find the podcast on YouTube titled "Dr. Garry P. Nolan UFO Tucker Carlson Full Interview 03/08/2022." You will find it quite interesting. Dr. Nolan was never a believer in UFOs or paranormal activity; he needed the science to prove it. Well, after a visit from some federal government agents who wanted him to do some testing on military personnel who had encounters with an unknown object that caused severe physical and mental abnormalities, he became convinced of the evidence through MRIs that something was quite peculiar. He now speaks publicly regarding his findings. He stated in the interview, "They come from both out of space and here, under the earth, in the oceans." It is a fascinating podcast, and Nolan is a very credible and well-known Stanford University scientist. He warns people to stay away from any unknown crafts because they have caused permanent brain damage in the individuals tested. There is also, he stated, evidence of increased intuition and psychic ability in some of the people who claim they were abducted. Janet Russell, a psychic medium who passed away in April 2023, and Angela Heil, who took part in the ministry interviews for this book, claim they were abducted.

Many Christian leaders around the world claim that aliens are the fallen angels from the first earth age. If you do a search on ancient aliens or fallen angels on YouTube, you will find many preachers and podcasters discussing this topic. Since Tucker Carlson left Fox News, he has aired more podcasts on various programs discussing the slow government release of information, what they aren't telling the public about, and perhaps what we should all be concerned about in the future. Some say that these aliens are a distraction for the Rapture of the church: everyone who isn't taken up to God's kingdom before the appearance of the Antichrist will believe that those who were taken up were taken by aliens instead. Why would they do that? To further discredit God and the word of Jesus Christ that He will save his elect. Whether the Rapture comes at the beginning, middle, or end of the tribulation (which then would be at the time of the Second Coming), only God knows. Roman Catholics have testified on many podcasts that it will be at the end; however, many believe it will be at the beginning or middle, while other ministries don't believe in it at all. I will get further into this discussion in the next chapter.

Let's hear the Christian viewpoints on these topics.

Father Claret:

- "The church has not made a statement regarding UFO sightings, aliens, or the books of Enoch."
- "The Roman Catholic Church never had the books of Enoch in its Bible."

Reverend Bustillos:

- "Demons are not just the fallen angels.'
- "The fallen angels are the strongest demons—with Lucifer being the top demon."
- "The Giants that scientists are discovering the remains of are Nephilim—and they were not destroyed in the first earth age."
- "They were not created by God but by the fallen angels and therefore do still roam the earth."
- "The Nephilim are the disembodied spirits of the Giants."
- "There are hybrids on the earth all over [that] were present at the time of the flood."
- He believes that the term *Guf* is not biblical.
- He states, "We are given one life." He does not believe in reincarnation. He believes that is the devil's way of playing tricks on people.

Reverend Pennella:

- "The UFOs that we see can be good angels or bad angels."
- He believes "they could be from other planets—it's unknown."
- He claims he does have the books of Enoch but does not read or refer to them in scripture.
- He does believe "all souls were created at once, referencing Isaiah 49:1–2: "The Lord called me before I was born, while I was in my mother's womb."
- He believes our souls were created before the creation of the earth.

Reverend Boggs:

- "It is not truly possible to know for sure what happened in the first earth age."
- He believes the earth to be 14 billion years old, where young church fathers interpret the earth's age according to the book of Genesis, to have been created in literally six days.
- He believes the Guf to be a mystical Jewish belief but one that is quite fascinating to think about.
- "It is impossible to know for sure if we were preincarnate souls and whether we were created at once or were created over time."
- "The important factor is that we ought to be concerned about is living our life like Christ."
- "Eastern Orthodox religion teaches that there is only one life." However, Reverend Boggs claims he has met many people in his life whom he felt he had met before and has had many déjà vu experiences, especially when he was younger. His training in Zen Buddhist communities has led him to believe that "we live many lifetimes, until we eventually come to the fullness of truth and unite ourselves fully to the Source, at which point we stop being born into human bodies."
- Regarding UFOs and fallen angels, Reverend Boggs says, "It is possible that some aliens may be the fallen angels."
- He is "quite aware" of the array of aliens identified, including the grays and reptilians. He believes the reptilians are most likely the species that has enslaved humanity and are the origins of the Satan figure, who appeared as a snake in the garden of Eden.
- He states, "the grays come in small and large versions and are noted as those that crashed at Roswell." To Reverend Boggs' knowledge, 'they are using human DNA to try and give themselves a new life, as they are very advanced and used cloning for so long that they are now dying, unable to clone themselves any longer. They are creating human hybrids to try and save their race."
- The Nephilim, according to Reverend Boggs, "were thought to be half-angel, half-human hybrid giants brought about by fallen angels (demons) who had mated with human women." He added, "I believe these were possibly some members of the ancient Anunnaki race, which came from the planet Nibiru, according to Sitchin."

Reverend Krahn:

- Regarding the book of Enoch, he said, "I did not follow it and was not aware of the first earth age Bible study on the top of the Guf."
- He did mention the Apocrypha in that it had not been accepted into the Bible.
- Regarding UFO sightings or other paranormal activity, he stated, "We really don't know—anything is possible."
- In reference to psychic energy, he believes "spirit is the life-force energy from God."
- "It's the element of our being, but to stay focused on God—as to not be misled."

Reverend Hartman:

- He believes the book of Enoch is real; however, he does not preach about it. "It is not discussed in Baptist ministry."
- As far as paranormal activity, he states that "the Bible warns to stay away from it as it may be of the devil."
- Reverend Hartman does "recognize the gifts that come from psychic ability," but he stated, "You don't know where the source is coming from."
- He was "not aware of the 'Guf' as written in the book of Enoch and in ancient Hebrew texts," but he did say, "Our soul as stated in the book of Jeremiah 1:5: "I already knew you before you were in your mother's womb."
- Regarding the UFOs and whether ancient aliens are fallen angels, he said he believes so.

Reverend Heil:

- "I have been abducted by aliens on several occasions."
- She believes that they are the fallen angels such as referenced in the book of Enoch or the first earth age.
- "They are present on the earth—still here." She says she's seen all of them—the grays, reptilians, green/silver humanoids, and so on.

TAKING INVENTORY

1. Had you ever heard of the first Earth age before reading this chapter?
2. Were you aware of the books of Enoch?
3. Had you ever heard of the term Guf before?
4. What do you think of ancient aliens?
5. Do you believe ancient aliens are the fallen angels?
6. What are your thoughts on the Giants and their relation to the Nephilim?
7. Do you have any thoughts on what the governments around the world know or don't know?
8. Can you explain stories of people missing time and being abducted?
9. What are your thoughts on what happened at Roswell, the famous UFO crash? Or is it conspiracy theory?
10. How do you think these stories relate to the Bible?

Twelve

THE RAPTURE AND THE SECOND COMING

Then I saw a new heaven and a new earth. The former heaven and
the former earth had passed away, and the sea was no more.
— Revelation 21:1

The Rapture and Second Coming of Christ has been a topic of conversation since Christ died on the cross. It is believed that even the apostles perhaps thought the Second Coming of Jesus would occur during their lifetime. The signs of the end times have been closely studied and observed for centuries. Many prophets have come and gone, and we as humans still ponder upon when that day will occur. Are we now at the end of time? Are the signs here, or are they merely the birth pains leading to decades or perhaps centuries to go?

As you will hear, some Christian ministers believe the Rapture will occur in the beginning of the tribulation, while others believe it will be in the middle or the end of the tribulation. And yet others don't believe in the Rapture at all. You will have the opportunity to read about their personal opinions or those of the churches they serve in. Let's take a look at what's happening in the world now that is different from the past and what religious leaders, scientists, scholars, prophets, and visionaries are saying.

In a recap of chapter 4, I mentioned that the book of Revelation speaks of the end of times and what signs to look for, and it says there will be an illumination of consciousness and awakening prior to the miracle as the Blessed Mother told Conchita Gonzalez in a small village in Garabandal of northern Spain—one of the four children during the apparitions of the Blessed Mother in northern Spain in the years 1961–1965. Conchita is still alive today, and the illumination of consciousness is to occur soon, she claims. At that time all souls on the earth will learn and be fully aware that Jesus Christ is the Messiah, the Son of God; they will also be shown their consciousness in view of the Lord, which will be truthful on all levels of their good deeds and sins and their relationship to Jesus Christ. People will have no question as to who Christ is, and moreover they will clearly see their sins and how their energy and contributions affected those around them and the world at large. This event will mark a time when we will be close to the Second Coming of Christ. It will be a time of great peace, but it will not last long—only long enough for people to turn their lives around before the chastisements of the Lord. After this there will be a great sign in the sky, illuminating for all to see the symbol of the Lord's presence. This sign will be present to the end of this age. This earth age will then end, and a new, third earth age will begin. Not all Christian religions follow this vision or belief. There are many skeptics and varying interpretations of the end of times and what that phrase means. According to Conchita, this sign or miracle will occur in the same village in Spain where the apparitions appeared in the early 1960s. This sign will be illuminated across the globe, so no matter where you live, you will see it in the sky. You can read more about this miracle and the illumination of consciousness in Xavier Reyes-Ayral's book *Revelations: The Hidden Secret Messages and Prophecies of the Blessed Virgin Mary*. There is enormous information in this text that will be valuable for the end times. Reyes-Ayral identifies in detail the apparitions of La Salette, of La Fraudais, of Tilly, of Fatima, of Akita, of Garabandal, of Medjugorje, and of the pope, saints, and mystics. All of these apparitions have foretold events that have happened or will happen; however, many of the chastisements can be delayed or stopped with prayer and with a return of our nations to faith in Christ. Reyes-Ayral has discussed his research and book on many Christian platforms, including Dr. Taylor Marshall's YouTube channel, Joe McClane's YouTube channel Mother and Refuge of the End Times, Austin Macauley Publishers' YouTube podcast, Dr. Christine Bacon's YouTube channel, and more. Reyes-Ayral goes over in detail what is yet to come, especially returning to the apparitions at Garabandal, through messages of Conchita Gonzalez as indicated above.

The miracles and apparitions of Fatima in 1917 involved three shepherd children at Cova da Iria in Fatima, Portugal—Lucia dos Santos, Francisco, and Jacinta Marto—who had visions of the Blessed Mother. Sister Lucia published memoirs of two secrets that came from the Virgin Mary; a third was revealed to the Catholic church in 1960. As a reminder, you can listen to updates regarding Fatima's messages on YouTube as well as find many published books regarding these apparitions and miracles that happen there. The secrets that were revealed future events that would occur, including wars, natural disasters, or events that have since happened as revealed or will soon happen. Hundreds of thousands of people still make pilgrimages to Fatima to witness miracles in the sky and to see this holy place. These messages are from the Blessed Mother to pray because the sins of the world are worse now than ever in history. God will not allow evil to continue, and many people, including many of God's children if they don't turn back to Christ, will be condemned to hell for eternity.

Another book speaking to the end times is *The End of the Present World* by Father Charles Arminjon. In it, Arminjon talks about a Christian's sacrifice and the means to redemption. He goes into detail about the end times and the signs that will precede it as written in the book of Revelation. He talks about the persecution by the Antichrist and the conversion of the Jews—by the way, some feel this includes the Gentiles too as they were all Christ's followers. Some have lost their faith, but in the end, they will reclaim it. Father Arminjon states in his book that *universal judgment* is the last scene of the drama here on the earth. It is the fulfillment of all partial judgments on humankind that emanated from God's justice, and it will be done on an individual basis. However, the end won't be the end; it will be a new beginning with God's reign on earth.

As for the exact hour, no one knows it, neither the angels in heaven nor the Son, but the Father only. (Matthew 24:36)

Father Arminjon states that Christ tells us that the afflictions and prodigies of nature, which will mark the latter ages of humankind, are prelude to and the beginning of still greater sorrows. This is referred to as *early birth pangs*. He goes on to emphasize to his readers that the signs today are the same signs that occurred in ancient times, and experience shows that they are insufficient to prove the proximity of the judgment. There are three signs, however, that will foreshadow the end of time, referring to Matthew 24:14.

1. The good news of the kingdom will be proclaimed throughout the world as a witness to all nations.
2. The appearance of the man of sin, the Antichrist.
3. The conversion of the Jewish people, who will adore Lord Jesus and recognize Him as the promised Messiah.

Ned Dougherty, writer of *Fast Lane to Heaven*, saw an apparition of the Blessed Mother at the Eastport Shrine, Long Island. In his book, he speaks about his NDE, during which he went gone in and out of consciousness after having a heart attack. He proclaims he visited heaven after calling out to Jesus at the time of his heart attack. He felt himself falling into what he thought would be hell, what he felt only to be complete darkness, until he saw God's light bringing him back up into the kingdom of heaven. His book describes in great detail all the things he had seen and who he met. Upon his journey in heaven, he was shown the future. Ned had his NDE in 1984 but didn't write his book until the 1990s, and it was published in 2001. He states God had prepared His plan for the future of all humankind, and it includes the following:

1. "A Global Spiritual Awakening that will be unparalleled in the history of humanity." It will be experienced by every single soul on the earth; it will be a worldwide spiritual and supernatural event.
2. "A protective mantle upon the Earth. In God's own words: "I will pour out My Spirit on all of mankind!" (This sounds similar to Conchita's messages from the Blessed Mother.)
3. "Miracles and Healings. An unprecedented number of miraculous and supernatural events will occur throughout the world,

particularly beatific visions, and apparitions. Healers who are filled with the Holy Spirit will perform miraculous healings, both spiritual and physical."

4. "Cataclysmic Events. Depending on mankind's response to God, these events may be altered, postponed, or canceled."

Dougherty says, "How to respond to God's calling? Just pray and meditate, and we will begin to recognize and work with God's plan." He was shown many personal as well as global events that would occur, and some were remarkably true.

The Lady of the Light showed him the following future global events:

1. "Major events would occur in the Middle East and then Italy."
2. "A terrorist attack in Italy, specifically Rome, and it would be directed against one world leader."
3. "Terrorist attacks and acts of war and aggression will continue to plague the Middle East, Africa, and Europe."
4. "Wars and rumors of wars will continue to plague the Eastern Hemisphere, spreading from the Middle East into Africa and Europe, and then to countries of the former Soviet Union and to the Far East, particularly China."
5. "The greatest threat to global peace and preservation will come from China, which is preparing for a global war and domination by building the largest army in the world, prophetically referred to in the book of Revelation as the army of 'two hundred million.'" The Lady of the Light told Dougherty to pray for the conversion of China. This conversion is key to the salvation of the world.
6. The Western Hemisphere will be spared most of the acts of terrorism and war; however, Dougherty was told that a major attack would befall New York City or Washington, DC, severely impacting the way we live in the United States. (Now this book was written before 9/11—keep that in mind.)
7. "The Western Hemisphere will be plagued by mainly natural disasters. Freakish, erratic, unreasonable weather patterns will create severe tidal flooding and land erosion. There will be devastating tornadoes and windstorms; severe winter conditions

with record snowfalls and freezing temperatures; record summer heat waves with severe drought; and an increase in destructive storms and hurricanes."

8. "The financial and banking institutions will collapse due in large part to the failure of the insurance companies as a result of natural disasters. The United States will be thrown into political, economic, and social chaos."

9. "The US government will fail to meet its financial obligations as a result of its staggering natural debt and will collapse. As a result of the destruction of US military bases from natural disasters, the United States will lose its ability to wage war or defend itself, leaving the country vulnerable to invasion by foreign troops, particularly by China's 'army of two hundred million.'"

10. "Shadowy and publicly unknown world figures will attempt to establish a 'new world order' by creating a worldwide government supposedly for the benefit of humanity.... They will attempt to reorganize the world's financial and banking system in a manner that will permit unelected leaders to manipulate and control the future of the world for their own personal benefit and gain. Their greed for wealth and lust will motivate them, and they will create a secular and materialistic world devoid of individual freedoms."

11. "There will be a shifting of the Earth's axis, creating dramatic climate changes and possibly resulting in massive earthquakes, volcanic eruptions, and huge tidal waves on both the east and west coasts of the United States, as well as around the world."

12. "There will be a great shift in the location of the populated areas as a result of both the geophysical and geopolitical changes. Coastal and other low-lying and unstable areas will diminish in population, while mountainous and other stable areas will become more desirable. Spiritually minded people will be drawn together to create new self-supporting communities and self-sustaining communities. These pioneers of vision who are attuned to God's plan for humankind will be the architects for the brave new world that God has envisioned for our future."

The book of Revelation speaks all about the end times, specifying what will happen first and the order in which to expect these things to occur. Many find the book of Revelation to be merely symbolic, while others take it literally; the Roman Catholic Church claims it is both symbolic and literal text. The apostles themselves spoke of the end times, as did other texts from the Old and New Testament. It's in the books of Enoch and has been discussed by visionaries and prophets around the world. Many people are having Rapture dreams, as published on YouTube and in many texts. I, myself, had a Rapture dream—I have to say it seemed amazingly real. I don't doubt at all that messages come from heaven across the veil. Jesus reassured us not to be afraid of these times but to be watchful and always ready to meet our Lord, Jesus Christ. Only the elect, who have cherished and worshipped Jesus, will be raptured up. The remainder will have to turn to Christ before the Second Coming or judgment day to be saved. I always hold onto hope that people will do that. Remember to pray—praying the Rosary is very powerful. Don't lead a dark life. Always look for goodness in the world, be charitable, forgive so that you might be forgiven, and ask God all the time to forgive your sins. We are only human, and human nature is to sin. It's the mortal sins we most definitely need to confess to keep our pathway to heaven open and aligned with Jesus Christ. We are saved by His grace, but that does not mean we are not responsible for our sin.

According to the book of Revelation, there will be wars and rumors of wars—but that still won't be the end. He will come like a thief in the night; people will be dancing and marrying, bearing children, and going to work. He will come when we least expect Him. The Antichrist will rise halfway through the tribulation period. Although there have been many antichrists—those who don't follow Jesus Christ are antichrists—but the book of Revelation refers to "the Antichrist"—the evil one who will take over the world and fool many people. He will claim to be the Messiah, but he is not. He will have the number 666 in his name or title, and he will enforce a chip or mark on the forehead or hand to buy or sell goods in the end days. Jesus promised to shorten those days because, if He didn't, no one would survive. Jesus wants all God's children to return to heaven with Him by our free will given to us by God. Many earthly disasters, diseases, and climate changes will take place—they are the birth pangs of things to come. The end will be near when these things become progressive in nature and the disasters do not let up—these are the signs that the end is very near. People will flee to the mountains or caves for protection, but there will be no protection for those who don't follow Him. The earth will ultimately be on fire with wars, ending with the battle of Armageddon. Watch what is happening in Israel; God will not allow Israel to be taken over. That will be a telling sign.

As for what to expect after the Second Coming, Jesus Christ will choose His elect, the saved. According to scripture and Christian interpretation, Christ will rule for one thousand years, during which time there will be profound peace on the earth, free of sickness and sin. Those who are sinful and are not saved will be bound to Hades until judgment day. After that day will be the second death, our eternal soul's fate. A new heaven and a new earth—one far better than the life we are used to now—will be established. We will have nothing to be afraid of as He promised. Just follow Jesus Christ and accept Him as your Lord and Savior. Interpretations from Christian viewpoints vary on what this looks like, but the focus is to trust in God, to follow Jesus Christ and His teachings, and to lead a good life. Avoid any and all dark energy and demonic actions that can lead you astray. Jesus Christ says, "I will come quickly" … "like a thief in the night." Always be ready. Confess your sins, be forgivable, and love others like Christ has loved you. This is a very brief summary of the book of Revelation. I highly recommend that you read directly from the Bible, and please refer to the book of Revelation for further detail. I also highly recommend the New American Standard Bible (NASB) or the King James Bible. This scripture written by apostle Peter in the NASB provides a good description of what to expect.

> Beloved, this is now the second letter I am writing to you in which I am stirring up your sincere mind by way of a reminder, to remember the words spoken beforehand by the holy prophets and the commandment of the Lord and Savior spoken by your apostles.

The Coming Day of the Lord

> Know first of all that in the last days mockers will come with their mocking, following after their own lusts, and saying, "Where is the promise of His coming? For ever

since the fathers fell asleep, all things continue just as they were from the beginning of creation." For when they maintain this, it escapes their notice that by the word of God the heavens existed long ago and the earth was formed out of water and by water, through which the world at that time was destroyed by being flooded with water. But by His word the present heavens and earth are being reserved for fire, kept for the day of judgment and destruction of ungodly people.

But do not let this one fact escape your notice, beloved, that with the Lord one day is like a thousand years, and a thousand years like one day. The Lord is not slow about His promise, as some count slowness, but is patient toward you, not willing for any to perish, but for all to come to repentance.

A New Heaven and Earth

But the day of the Lord will come like a thief, in which the heavens will pass away with a roar and the elements will be destroyed with intense heat, and the earth and its works will be discovered.

Since all these things are to be destroyed in this way, what sort of people ought you to be in holy conduct and godliness, looking for and hastening the coming of the day of God, because of which the heavens will be destroyed by burning, and the elements will melt with intense heat! But according to His promise we are looking for new heavens and a new earth, in which righteousness dwells.

Therefore, beloved, since you look for these things, be diligent to be found spotless and blameless by Him, at peace, and regard the patience of our Lord as salvation; just as also our beloved brother Paul, according to the wisdom given him, wrote to you, as also in all his letters, speaking in them of these things, in which there are some things that are hard to understand, which the untaught and unstable distort, as they do also the rest of the Scriptures, to their own destruction. You therefore, beloved, knowing this beforehand, be on your guard so that you are not carried away by the error of unscrupulous people and lose your own firm commitment, but grow in the grace and knowledge of our Lord and Savior Jesus Christ. To Him be the glory, both now and to the day of eternity. Amen. (2 Peter 3, NASB)

If you want further clarification on what is to come, I recommend Xavier Reyes-Ayral's book *Revelations: The Hidden Secret Messages and Prophecies of the Blessed Virgin Mary*. In it, Reyes-Ayral outlines much of what is to come through visionaries Conchita of Garabandal, and St. Padre Pio. It provides insight into many visionaries and what has come true across the years. Reyes-Ayral is often seen on podcasts on YouTube providing updates to the messages given to Conchita. Another author, Tim Cohen, wrote a book I highly recommend: *The Antichrist and a Cup of Tea*. Cohen goes into much detail of how we can identify the Antichrist—who he is and how his number adds to 666—and Cohen has repeatedly testified that King Charles is that Antichrist. Cohen claims that his research is undeniably true and is certain of his findings. You can listen to his interviews with podcasters on YouTube—just do a search on Tim Cohen. You can also purchase his book through his publishing company, Prophecy House.

Let's hear what the Christian leaders have to say about the end times, the Rapture of the church, and the Second Coming of Christ.

Father Claret:

- "There is no Rapture of the church."
- "The term *Rapture* is not recognized in the Catholic church."
- Father Claret emphasizes that the Eucharist—the receiving of the body and blood of Jesus Christ—is our so-called Rapture. We are one with God in the Eucharist.
- "As far as the Second Coming, always be ready."

- "The church won't identify signs of the Second Coming such as the mark of the beast unless it is confirmed by God Himself. It must be clearly evident and not mistaken for the church to announce it."
- "The church sees the book of Revelation as both symbolic and literal."
- "Much of the text is spoken in parables."
- "The church has not yet spoken on being in the end of times." … "It is not yet identified."
- When questioned regarding the apparitions of the Blessed Mother by Conchita Gonzalez in Garabandal, Spain, he said that he did not know of those apparitions.
- Father Claret did say that "the church has accepted the famous warnings in Fatima." He also stated that "there have been thousands of warnings of the end of times; some have been accepted, some were not."

Reverend Bustillos:

- "All I have to say is that demons are much worse in the past five years than any other time of my career."
- He believes we may be in the beginning of the tribulation period.
- He does not follow any visionaries; however, he does believe we will have a Rapture and things are getting worse.
- He wanted to add that "demons don't leave people alone without an exorcism."
- "If you don't believe in Jesus Christ, you are automatically a disciple of the devil—the devil owns your soul."
- He stated, "The Jews follow the old covenant, where Christians follow the new covenant. Those that don't follow the new covenant are not saved."

Reverend Pennella:

- He believes "there will be a Rapture before the tribulation period."
- He does feel we are in the end of times.

- Although he has heard of visionaries such as the miracles at Fatima, he does not follow them.
- He follows scripture and believes we are on the threshold of the tribulation period.

Reverend Krahn:

- "We are in the end times—there have been touchstones to suggest these things need to happen before Christ comes again."
- Although he mentions we have heard in the past that others thought on a certain date the Second Coming would happen and the time passed, he says, "The return of Christ will be a surprise, but the signs are here."
- He did not seem to have an opinion or belief one way or the other on the Rapture other than to say, "It is possible because there was some context in scripture to allude to that; however, it is not consistent."

Reverend Boggs:

- "There is no Rapture period."
- "This is a term popularized by the late John Nelson Darby in the late 1800s and has never been believed in or accepted by Orthodox Christians."
- He claims that "none of the early church fathers taught or believed in Rapture, and this is nothing more than a Western idea."
- "We have technically been in the end of time since Christ ascended into heaven."
- Eastern Orthodox Christians see "the signs of the end times as more of a metaphor than literal signs—although we may be witnessing certain signs as depicted in the Bible."
- "Eastern Orthodox Christians claim to read the Bible more symbolically, than literally like Protestants."
- "Not everything in scripture is to be taken literally."
- "To interpret the signs as meaning the tribulation is here is incorrect."

Reverend Hartman:

- "We are at the end of time."
- He feels the detailed signs are humankind's ability to clone humans and animals, what's happening in nature—our weather patterns are changing—and the different agendas of sin accessibility."
- He believes the Rapture of the church will occur right before the mark of the beast— "halfway through the tribulation."
- He stated that he had heard of the apparitions of Conchita of Gonzalez in Spain but not of Fatima. He did not have any further comment on them.

Reverend Heil:

- "It is possible we are in the end of times."
- She emphasized, "However, it's never too late. We can still be redeemed by faith in Christ."

TAKING INVENTORY

1. Do you believe in the Rapture of the church?
2. Do you believe the Rapture will be at the beginning, middle, or end of the tribulation?
3. Reflecting on the visionaries, do you feel they are real? Why or why not?
4. Do you believe in the Second Coming of Christ in the literal context?
5. Do you believe the book of Revelation is in literal or symbolic context, or both?
6. Do you believe in the resurrection of Christ?
7. Do you believe you are ready for the Second Coming of Christ and judgment day?

Thirteen

CONCLUSION AND SUMMARY

The one who gives this testimony says, "Yes, I am
coming soon." Amen! Come, Lord Jesus!
Revelation 22:20

The *Watching of the Lord* is because of God's love, according to Reverend
Boggs. The discussion of *faith* versus *belief* brought unanimous agreement
that those two terms do indeed mean something different. Almost all
of the Christian ministers I interviewed felt wholeheartedly that having
faith means having a deeper connection to God and requires more than
just belief in God. Good deeds do matter, but as Christians, the belief is
that salvation comes only through faith in Christ. Our faith is what saves
us, our faith is what heals us, and our faith is what drives us to do good
deeds. Our purpose is to serve Him, say the ministers. We are Christians
of faith, and through our faith we serve Him. We all have our unique gifts,
and we bring our own individuality to this earth to make it a better place.
That is our purpose.

All Christian ministers believe salvation comes through Jesus Christ and that there are consequences for not living a good life. All claim that you must confess your sins before God, and only God provides the grace of forgiveness. They all believe that, without remorse, there is no forgiveness, and we must repent to be saved. Blasphemy of the Holy Spirit was unanimously agreed to be the only unforgivable sin—it refers to rejecting the Father, the Son, and the Holy Spirit and not accepting Jesus Christ as Lord and Savior upon death.

They all believe we can be redeemed by our sins through remorse and repentance. We must have remorse to gain forgiveness, and we must *make an attempt* not to do that sin again. The Catholic church has a sacrament of reconciliation; the forgiveness, they say, is given by God. Unlike other Christian ministers, however, the priest made a point to further explain that we are bound by our sins if someone else doesn't forgive us and we don't forgive another. Confessing to another in scripture can rectify that. In my opinion, confessing to another person, such as a minister or priest, also provides a larger scale release of built-up guilt. It is a cleansing of the soul. To be forgiven by someone else in the body does help with remorse—not to forget the lesson but to let it go, to move forward, and to lead a better life. From my interview with the Roman Catholic priest, this did become clearer to me as I was unsure of the reason to confess to a priest as opposed to directly to God alone. I have been a Catholic all my life but was never clear on why we needed to confess to a priest when God Himself does the forgiving. Now I understand.

About half of the ministers and clergy agreed that abortion is equal to the murder of an adult; however, nearly all who didn't agree with that said it should only be done in extreme cases—that it is *not* to be taken lightly. They all seemed to identify with mortal versus venial sins; however, regardless of the sin, all agreed it needs to be confessed *in order to be* forgiven by Christ. Even the smallest of sins can steer us away from Christ.

In St. Augustine's book *Confessions*, he writes, "No one can lose you, my God, unless he forsakes you.... And, if he abandons your love his only refuse is your wrath.... Wherever he turns, he will find your law to punish him, for your law is the truth and the truth is yourself." In the end it is only *you* that destroys yourself. This understanding is profound in understanding sin and why God would allow it on the earth if He loved us so. Just ponder upon St. Augustine's insight for a moment after reading through the ministers' responses on sin—understanding that *you* are your own worst enemy. *We choose our lives; we choose God, or we reject Him. It is as simple as that. Anything void of God is darkness. Where God is not present, goodness does not exist.*

Only about half were aware of the new drug adrenochrome and its impact on child sex trafficking, sex crimes, and abortion or torture. Some still aren't certain whether it is a conspiracy theory, or it is truly happening. In my personal commentary, I'd like to add that the dreadful crimes that occur across the globe have an impact on our society's values, morals, and choices and do undoubtedly contribute to more serious crimes and sin. The use of adrenochrome is a relatively new topic of conversation; it may have been around, but the idea of this evil act being implemented—and for one of the leading motivations of child sex trafficking and abductions—is very scary. There are so many horrible things going on in this world that we don't ever want to think about. However, the more we look away and leave the response to someone else, the more our morals dissipate. Greed takes control, and people are exposed to extreme physical, emotional, and sexual abuse. I believe people need to always be alert for anything that doesn't seem right. In health care, the saying is "If you see something, say something." You could just save a life.

In the discussion of near-death experiences, many Christian ministers had heard of this phenomenon but still didn't know what to make of it. Most believe that the stories are truthful; it is not a matter of thinking these people are lying. In fact, research into NDEs has proved that consciousness does exist outside the body at least for a short period of time. The question is how it relates to scripture other than that we know after we pass there is eternal life in heaven or hell. There is nothing in the Bible saying that we can go to heaven and come back—this is the fascination of all these amazing stories. To me it adds proof to my hope that God gives even more chances to His children than we can imagine. He is endlessly merciful. God didn't give us all the answers, and perhaps we don't need to know everything—we just need to trust Him.

The stories of the books of Enoch seem to fascinate all; however, none of the ministers focus on that, only on the new covenant. Many were aware of visionaries and accounts of NDEs. Reverend Angela Heil, a nondenominational minister, claims she had two NDEs and believes that is how she got the gift of mediumship. She claims to be clairvoyant, clairaudient, and clairsentient—she also claims to be an empath and will channel Archangel Michael in readings. However, she was also abducted by aliens. She is certain that they are evil; however, she is unsure of where they come from or if they indeed are the fallen angels.

Father Claret stated, "We don't know the day or the hour—and the church will identify the time when they are certain it is here." The church doesn't want to mislead the congregation. Pastor Boggs stated, "We have technically been in the end of times since Jesus was resurrected from the dead." He also pointed out, "Not all information in the book of Revelation should be taken literally. Some of the literature written had symbolic interpretations."

The point of this book is to provide insight to those who may choose to be in the dark about ongoing societal issues lying in the corners of this dark world, but if we continue to ignore these issues, more people will get hurt. People do need to be aware of their actions and the actions of others and how they impact society at large. We are on this earth to learn, to lead good lives, to have a relationship with our creator, and to serve Him and others.

Take time to go back and reflect on the questions at the end of each chapter. Reflect on the information that has been stated and share this awareness with others so we can all be better informed and make better choices that align with Jesus Christ.

God bless all of you. My hope is that we all choose Jesus Christ and return one day to meet in God's heavenly kingdom as one united family!

Fourteen

AFFIRMATIONS, THE ROSARY, AND PRAYERS

> At your name they rejoice all day, and through
> your justice they are exalted.
> — Psalms 89:17

We are saved by grace in faith, but good deeds are testimony to our faith.

God is your boss; everyone else is just playing a role in your life. Be mindful of the characters of those from whom you are taking your orders.

Do not neglect the gift you were given.

You must learn from every offense, or the lesson will repeat.

Sin is only forgivable with repentance and remorse.

Reconciliation only happens if forgiveness has happened.

Allowing someone to victimize you is never OK.

Once you recognize abuse or witness it, it has become your responsibility to stop it.

You are the judge of the circumstances you tolerate; God is the judge of their fate.

The only unforgivable sin is blasphemy to the Holy Spirit.

Learn to love yourself first, then you can learn to love others.

Be patient and kind to others, and that will be returned to you.

Don't be envious of others. You have your own gifts—cherish them.

Jealousy is a wasted energy; focus on the gifts God gave you and your service to God.

Stop evil in its tracks, no matter the cost.

Money is not worth the cost of love and respect, and it will never bring you happiness.

Greed is the goal of the devil; be mindful of whom you follow.

Idolize only Jesus Christ, our Lord and Savior. No one else can save you.

Aromatherapy, crystals, yoga, Reiki, Pilates, and other alternative therapies are wonderful for anxiety—but never use them in a ritualistic format. Be aware of your intention and keep Jesus Christ as your first and foremost aid in recovery.

Remember, we are all sinners. No one is perfect, but it does take recognition of our sins and reconciliation with remorse of the hurt we caused to grow in spirit and be forgiven by our eternal Father in the end.

God bless you on this journey of life.

HOW TO PRAY THE HOLY ROSARY

Pray The Glory Be & The Fatima Prayer

Pray 10 Hail Marys, meditating on the 3rd Mystery

Pray The Glory Be & The Fatima Prayer

Third Mystery

Announce the Fourth Mystery, & Pray The Our Father

Announce the Third Mystery, & Pray The Our Father

Pray 10 Hail Marys, meditating on the 4th Mystery

Fourth Mystery

Second Mystery

Pray 10 Hail Marys, meditating on the 2nd Mystery

Announce the Fifth Mystery, & Pray The Our Father

Announce the Second Mystery, & Pray The Our Father

Pray The Glory Be & The Fatima Prayer

Lastly, Pray The Hail Holy Queen

Pray The Glory Be & The Fatima Prayer

Fifth Mystery

First Mystery

Pray 10 Hail Marys, meditating on the 5th Mystery

Pray 10 Hail Marys, meditating on the 1st Mystery

Pray The Glory Be & The Fatima Prayer

Announce the First Mystery, & Pray The Our Father

Pray The Glory Be

Pray 3 Hail Marys for the gift of Faith, Hope, and Love

- Pray The Our Father

- Make the Sign of the Cross, & Pray The Creed.

MYSTERIES OF THE ROSARY

JOYFUL MYSTERIES
Happy times in the Lives of Jesus and Mary
1. The Annunciation
2. The Visitation
3. The Nativity of Jesus
4. The Presentation
5. Finding Jesus in the Temple

GLORIOUS MYSTERIES
These Mysteries show the Divinity of Jesus
1. The Resurrection
2. The Ascension
3. The Descent of the Holy Spirit
4. The Assumption of Mary
5. The Coronation of Mary

SORROWFUL MYSTERIES
Sad moments in the Lives of Jesus and Mary
1. The Agony in the Garden
2. The Scourging at the Pillar
3. The Crowning with Thorns
4. The Way of the Cross
5. The Crucifixion

LUMINOUS MYSTERIES
These recall times in Jesus' Life when He revealed God's Kingdom
1. The Baptism of Jesus
2. The First Miracle at Cana
3. The Proclamation of the Kingdom
4. The Transfiguration
5. The Institution of the Eucharist

The Apostles' Creed

I believe in God,
the Father almighty,
Creator of heaven and earth,
and in Jesus Christ, his only Son, our Lord,
who was conceived by the Holy Spirit,
born of the Virgin Mary,
suffered under Pontius Pilate,
was crucified, died and was buried;
he descended into hell;
on the third day he rose again from the dead;
he ascended into heaven,
and is seated at the right hand of God the Father almighty;
from there he will come to judge the living and the dead.
I believe in the Holy Spirit,
the holy catholic church,
the communion of saints,
the forgiveness of sins,
the resurrection of the body,
and life everlasting.
Amen.

The Our Father

Our Father, who art in heaven,
hallowed be thy name;
thy kingdom come;
thy will be done on earth as it is in heaven.
Give us this day our daily bread;
and forgive us our trespasses
as we forgive those who trespass
against us;
and lead us not into temptation,
but deliver us from evil.
Amen

The Hail Mary

Hail Mary, full of grace, the Lord is with you;
blessed are you among women,
and blessed is the fruit of your womb, Jesus.
Holy Mary, Mother of God,
pray for us sinners
now and at the hour of our death.
Amen.

The Glory Be

Glory be to the Father, the Son, and the Holy Spirit;
as it was in the beginning, is now, and ever shall be,
world without end.
Amen.

The Hail Holy Queen

Hail, holy Queen, mother of mercy,
our life, our sweetness, and our hope.
To you we cry, poor banished children of Eve;
to you we send up our sighs,
mourning and weeping in this valley of tears.
Turn, then, most gracious advocate,
your eyes of mercy toward us;
and after this, our exile,
show unto us the blessed fruit of your womb, Jesus.
O clement, O loving, O sweet Virgin Mary.

https://www.usccb.org/prayers/prayers-rosary

REFERENCES AND RECOMMENDED READINGS

"Three Earth Ages." (2018). Bible Study for Life. https://biblestudyforlife. com/three_world_ages.htm

Alexander, Eben. 2012. *Proof of Heaven*. Simon & Schuster Publishing Co.

Anthony, Mark. 2017. *Evidence of Eternity*. MN: Llewellyn Publications.

Arminjon, Father Charles. 2008. *The End of the Present World*. Sophia Institute Press.

Benedict XVI. 2023. *What Is Christianity?* San Francisco: Ignatius Press.

Besteman, Marvin. 2012. *My Journey to Heaven*. Revell.

Bevilacqua, J. C. D., and C. Deputatus. 1976. *Key of Heaven: A Prayer Book for Catholics*. William J. Hirten, Co.

Bodine, Echo. 1999. *Echoes of the Soul*. New World Library.

Burke, John. 2015. *Imagine Heaven*. Baker Publishing Group.

Burpo, Todd. 2011. *Heaven Is for Real*. Harper Collins Publishing Co.

Burton, Neel. 2014. "The Psychology and Philosophy of Envy." *Psychology Today*.

Dougherty, Ned. 2001. *Fast Lane to Heaven*. Hampton Roads Publishing Co. Inc.

Dye, H. L. 2019. "Is Emotional Abuse As Harmful as Physical and/or Sexual Abuse?" *Journal of Child and Adolescent Trauma* 13 (4): 399-407. DOI: 10.1007/s40653-019-00292-y.

Dyer, Wayne. 2007. *Inspiration Your Ultimate Calling*. Hay House Inc.

Eadie, Betty J. 1992. *Embraced by the Light*. Golf Leaf Press Inc.

https://millennial-grind.com

https://www.ANF.org

https://www.prophecyhouse.com

https://www.theatlantic.com

https://www.thehill.com

https://www.themarchoflife.org

https://www.thewashingtonpost.com

https://www.usccb.org/prayers/prayers-rosary

https://www.worldhealth.org

https://www.youtube.com/

https://www.zodianz.com

Jankowski, Kelley. 2016. *An Army in Heaven*. New York: Page Publishing.

Jung, H., Herrenkohl, T. I., Lee, J. O., Klika, J. B., & Skinner, M. L. (2015). Effects of Physical and Emotional Child Abuse and Its Chronicity on Crime Into Adulthood. *Violence and victims, 30*(6), 1004–1018. https://doi.org/10.1891/0886-6708.VV-D-14-00071

Kolbaba, Scott J. 2016. *Physicians' Untold Stories*. Create Space, Independent Publishing.

Kopel J. (2019). Near-death experiences in medicine. *Proceedings (Baylor University. Medical Center), 32*(1), 163–164. https://doi.org/10.10 80/08998280.2018.1542478

Kreeft, Peter. 1990. *Everything You Ever Wanted to Know about Heaven*. San Francisco: Ignatius Press.

Krems, J. A., K. E. G. Williams, A. Aktipis, and D. T. Kenrick. 2021. "Friendship Jealousy: One Tool for Maintaining Friendships in the Face of Third-Party Threats?" Journal of Personality and Social Psychology 120 (4): 977–1012. https://doi.org/10.1037/ pspi0000311

Lazarus, Clifford. 2019. "Can Consciousness Exist Outside the Body?" *Psychology Today*.

Liu, H., J. Geng, and P. Yao. 2021. "Relationship of Leadership and Envy: How to Resolve Workplace Envy with Leadership—A Bibliometric Review Study." Journal *of* Intell*igence* 9 (3): 44. DOI: 10.3390/jintelligence9030044.

Longo, Pat. 2019. *The Gifts Beneath Your Anxiety*. Kensington Publishing Corp.

Lumpkin, Joseph. 2009. *The Lost Books of the Bible: The Great Rejected Texts*. AL: Fifth Estate Publishers.

Lumpkin, Joseph. 2011. *The Books of Enoch*, 2nd Edition. AL: Fifth Estate Publishers.

Mark, K. P., E. Janssen, and R. R. Milhausen. 2011. "Infidelity in Heterosexual Couples: Demographic, Interpersonal, and Personality-Related Predictors of Extradyadic Sex." Arch*ives of Sexual* Behavior 40 (5): 971–82. DOI: 10.1007/s10508-011-9771-z.

Matthews, Patrick. 2018. *Never Say Goodbye*. MN: Llewelyn Publications.

Myss, Caroline. 2002. *Sacred Contracts*. New York: Harmony Books.

Myss, Caroline. 2017. *Anatomy of the Spirit*. New York: Harmony Books.

Myss, Caroline. 2020. *Intimate Conversations with the Divine*. Hay House Inc.

Neal, Mary. 2012. *To Heaven and Back*. Random House Publishing Co.

Neal, Mary. 2017. *7 Lessons from Heaven*. Random House Publishing Co.

New American Bible, St. Joseph Edition. 1986. Catholic Book Publishing Co.

Privilegio, Cum. 2019. *The Apocrypha*. Cambridge Press.

Reyes-Ayral, Xavier. 2022. *Revelations: The Hidden Secret Messages and Prophecies of the Blessed Virgin Mary*. Austin McCauley Publishers, LLC.

Russo, Kim. 2020. *Your Soul Purpose: Learn How to Access the Light Within*. HarperCollins Publishers.

Saint Augustine and R. S. Pine-Coffin. 1961. *St. Augustine's Confessions*. Penguin Books.

Shiyu, W., J. Weipeng, Z. Weniwei, et al. 2023. "Greed Personality Trait Links to Negative Psychopathology and Underlying Neural Substrates," Social Cognitive and Associative Neuroscience 18, no. 1.

Smith Jones, Susan. 1992. *Choose to Live Peacefully*. Celestial Arts Publishing.

Spellman, Francis J. 1943. *The Rosary, Roses of Prayer—From the Queen of Heaven*. W. H. Litho Co.

United Conference of Catholic Bishops website. https://www.usccb.org/prayers/prayers-rosary

Van Praag, James and Virtue, Doreen. 2013. *How to Heal a Grieving Heart*. Hay House Inc.

Van Praag, James and Virtue, Doreen. 2013. *Talking to Heaven Medium Cards*. Hay House Inc.

Van Praag, James. 2014. *The Souls Journey Lesson Cards*. Hay House, Inc.

www.bishopaccountability.org

Yang, C., and R. Tang. 2021. "Validating the 'Two Faces' of Envy: The Effect of Self-Control." Front*iers in* Psychology 12. DOI: 10.3389/fpsyg.2021.731451.

Zukav, Gary. 1989. *The Seat of the Soul.* Simon & Schuster, Inc.

ABOUT THE AUTHOR

Diane Calabrese worked as a recreational therapist for over three decades in hospitals, nonprofits, public schools, and universities. Today, she is an adjunct professor at Florida International University, the author of two self-help books, a member of the Long Island Authors Group, and an active participant on holistic wellness platforms. For more about Diane and her books, visit dianecalabrese.com.

Printed in the United States
by Baker & Taylor Publisher Services